T0147152

Made Right
with
God
Mankind's Deepest Desire

*A Short Treatise
on the Theology of
Salvation and Its
Many Aberrations*

Douglas C. McIntosh M.D.

WESTBOW
PRESS®
A DIVISION OF THOMAS NELSON
& ZONDERVAN

WestBow Press books may be ordered through booksellers or by contacting:

WestBow Press
A Division of Thomas Nelson & Zondervan
1663 Liberty Drive
Bloomington, IN 47403
www.westbowpress.com
844-714-3454

ISBN: 978-1-6642-8168-4 (sc)
ISBN: 978-1-6642-8169-1 (hc)
ISBN: 978-1-6642-8167-7 (e)

Library of Congress Control Number: 2022919721

Print information available on the last page.

WestBow Press rev. date: 02/24/2023

Contents

Preface

Being made right with God has been the focus of so many people down through the ages, but the issue is, how can it become a reality in our lives, and how can we know for sure? This question is especially relevant when we see the multitude of answers, often contradictory to one another, that have been proposed. And how do we so often get it wrong when we've been given a divine guidebook, the Bible? It is good then at the beginning to give some reason why I would spend the time to write on this subject of salvation, about which more books have likely been written than any other. So many words, so many opinions! But the topic is, of course, critical to our eternal well-being.

In my short time here on earth, I have personally known numbers of people who were most likely true believers in the Lord Jesus but held beliefs that didn't seem to fully align with the character of the God they desired to follow. Nor did they seem to fully understand the greatness of what God was accomplishing when he created man in his own image. Nor lastly did they truly grasp the comprehensive nature of the salvation our Lord was procuring. It is for these reasons this paper has been written.

Very specifically these people would include those who believe God has provided his salvation for a select few he chose in a past eternity with all human choice removed. It would also include those who believe alternatively that in the end, everyone will be saved. There are some also who believe Calvary provided salvation, getting us, as it were, in the door; but then it is up to the individual to complete it by his or her good works. Also, I have talked with some who, despite having trusted in the Lord for salvation, believe it gives no guarantee of heaven since a person could lose his or her faith and be eternally lost or even just choose at some time to walk away from it and no longer believe. There are still others who feel they can believe in Christ yet at the same time still hold worldviews that include animist or pagan beliefs or more recently atheistic philosophies.

We must have a higher view of the greatness of our God beyond what we can even imagine and of the wonder of his creation, particularly of our humanity and especially of the exceeding greatness of his salvation. So I have attempted in this brief apology (a defense of Christian doctrine) to set out the biblical truth of this salvation from the Scriptures themselves as a template for us. And then I will seek to lay over it these other ideas or belief systems to see how they align. Let's be like the ancient Bereans, as Luke recorded in Acts, who "received the word with all eagerness, *examining the Scriptures daily to see if these things were so*" (Acts 17:11, emphasis added).

Despite this good start, many errors have crept into people's beliefs and understanding of this salvation being offered to us. To review, here is a short list of the more significant heresies seen during the nearly two-thousand-year history of the church age, giving us some obvious trends to be aware of.

Early

- Arianism (Jesus was the highest of all God's creation but not divine, thereby undermining the immutability of his character and the certainty and sufficiency of the salvation he provided.)
- Docetism/Gnosticism (Jesus's physical body was an illusion as was his crucifixion, so he didn't really die, leaving it up to us through the understanding of special knowledge to approach God.)
- Marcionism (The loving God of the New Testament was different from the wrathful One in the Old Testament, basically leading to polytheism.)
- Nestorianism (The man Jesus was wholly human and simply indwelt by God, making him finite and unfit to save us eternally from our sins.)

- Monophysitism (Christ was wholly divine, only appearing to be human and removing his ability to be the perfect mediator between God and man.)
- Pelagianism (The fall, while affecting Adam and Eve, wasn't passed on to us, so we still are able to choose to do good on our own.)

More Recent

- Jehovah's Witnesses or restorationists (Like Arianism, they deny belief in the Trinity, saying Jesus was God's created son but not God, although he shows us the way back to God and to a renewed earth; however, if we miss out, we simply cease to exist since there is no hell.)
- Christian Science (This modern form of Gnosticism teaches that the spiritual world is the only reality and is entirely good and that the material world—with its evil, sickness, and death—is an illusion; salvation is works based and dependent on believing right thoughts.)
- Mormonism (This religion, purported to be given by an angel, says that Jesus was a created being who was able over time to ascend to godhood through good works, which we all have the potential to do [see Revelation 22:18–19].)
- Unitarianism (This nontrinitarian belief system espouses a non-creedal universal salvation, having no formal core tenets essential to it.)

Almost without exception, heresies can be identified as systems of belief that accept unbiblical ideas regarding God and especially about the person and work of the Lord Jesus Christ. Many would have us believe that Jesus wasn't God or fully equal to God the Father or began as a man until he rose to godhood status. Others would say it's necessary for our salvation that human effort be added to the work of Christ, only begun at the cross. It's out of this belief that asceticism became so popular starting in the AD 400s and for many centuries after. Included in this was doing other great works such as pilgrimages during the Middle Ages, undertaken to ensure personal salvation.

Other, so-called Christian belief systems, such as Gnosticism, mentioned above, had a dualistic belief that all material things, including the body, were evil; only the spirit was good. Therefore, Christ couldn't have had a real body but just took on the appearance of one, with the implication that he didn't really die. But Hebrews 2 clearly tells us that the reason God the Son was incarnated as a man was so he could die! Our real goal in life, they would say then, is to rise progressively through an understanding of divine knowledge beyond what most people would be able to comprehend and so approach God in this way. It is ignorance of the heavenly sphere, they would say, not sin, from which we need to be saved. Paul fittingly calls this "being vain in their imaginations" (2 Corinthians 10:5 KJV). Finally, Pelagianism says that the fall didn't impart the sin nature to all mankind, just to Adam and Eve, so we still remain capable by our own will to choose to do good. In this view, Calvary becomes more of an example for us.

Some aberrations don't rise to the same level as those listed above since most of the people believing them are truly saved by the blood of Christ. They would have understood and believed Jesus died for their sins but in addition had attached to this, as Paul confesses to doing, the "the traditions of my fathers [i.e. of men]." (Galatians 1:14) Such would be Arminianism and Calvinism. Arminianism is very biblical in its understanding of the person of Christ and the plan of salvation except regarding sanctification and eternal security. Some of the denominations following this tradition would be Christian Reformed, Mennonite Brethren churches, Wesleyan churches, many Pentecostals, as well as Church of God and Church of the Nazarene. Here we see an excessive emphasis on man's free will on the one hand, and on the other, God's part in salvation, except for Jesus's death at Calvary, is downplayed. This inevitably leads to worrying about whether we believed the right way or whether, if we perhaps drift away from fellowship with God, we have lost our salvation, our relationship with him. This causes people in their uncertainty to lack real peace in their lives and to make repeated professions of salvation.

It is certainly true that when we are convicted of our sin, we must repent and accept the Lord Jesus Christ as our Savior. But salvation in its essence is all of God; we are, as John says a total of seven times in 1

John, "born of God" (1 John 3:9), and it is he who cleanses us from our sins because of Calvary when we turn to him in faith. He alone declares us righteous before the Father in heaven, and he indwells us with his Spirit, who also seals us for our guaranteed inheritance in heaven.

Calvinism also rejects most of these heretical notions listed previously above. Some of the denominations following this tradition would include Presbyterianism and others following what they would call the Reformed tradition. However, what this theological system of thought does is emphasize the complete sovereignty of God in the matter of salvation to the complete exclusion of human free will, which God created in us. They elevate God's holiness above all his other attributes of character including even his nature of love. This belief allows them to see God's love limited to the "all" he has chosen for salvation. God, they say, has provided salvation but limited it to, or made it available to, only those chosen by him in a past eternity without regard to human choice. Look at their own writings, called "A Faith to Confess," updated in 1997. This is the *Baptist Confession of 1689, Rewritten in Modern English* (Carey Publications, 1997. See point 3:5: "Before the world was made, God's eternal, immutable purpose, which originated in the secret counsel and good pleasure of His will, moved Him to Choose (or elect), in Christ, certain of mankind to everlasting glory. Out of His mere free grace and love He predestined these chosen ones to life, although there was nothing in them to cause Him to choose them."[1]

They teach that because of the complete spiritual blindness of the unsaved, those still in their sins would be unaware that they even were lost until regenerated by a sovereign act of God (although the large number of religions in the world trying to find a way back to God would give the lie to that). Then it is God, they say, who must impart in them even the ability, the faith, to accept this salvation. They believe in the biblical truth of eternal security, that people who are saved can never lose their salvation; but because of the blindness of the unsaved, they would say that people can also never really be sure they are one of the elect, the chosen. A misinterpretation of what James wrote would push them to continuously be doing work for God to reassure themselves of their salvation. So peace eludes them as well. See this passage: "Was not Abraham our father justified by works when he offered up his son Isaac on the altar? You see that faith was active along with his works, and faith was completed by his works; and the Scripture was fulfilled that says, 'Abraham believed God, and it was counted to him as righteousness'— and he was called a friend of God. You see that a person is justified by works and not by faith alone" (James 2:21–25).

Actually, James was simply saying (in the passage quoted above) that because of the new nature within the believer, the regenerated man *cannot help* but do the work of God. And indeed, others would be able to see the results of this new life in him as well.

Another troubling thing that's happening in the Christian faith more recently is the rise of a type of syncretism, taking the worldview the Creator God gave in Scripture but adding to it the worldview of naturalism, as espoused by the theory of evolution. *Syncretism* means mixing two opposing views of ultimate reality. This admixture has been seen many times before in animistic cultures, where Christian beliefs have simply been added rather than replacing the former belief system. Currently, naturalism is the popular belief that the material world— our earth and everything in it, including ourselves and the universe beyond—encompasses all reality. Nothing else exists, they would say, including God and the spiritual realm.

In our current age, we again see this mixing of beliefs happening and even creeping into the thinking of many Christians. What's being added, called "scientism," is a naturalistic philosophy that believes something is verifiably true only through the use of scientific principles and if it is in agreement with science, where, they would say, essential truth resides. In reality, however, science itself has continually had to update itself as new understanding replaces the old, so-called facts. This narrow view of the world takes account only of *natural* elements and forces, excluding the supernatural or spiritual. Therefore, whenever faith and science seem to be in conflict, science ought to win the day. After all, they say, doesn't faith really deal with feelings but science with facts? In reality, however, there is nothing so absolutely and unchangingly true as God's revelation to us in his Word. This type of naturalistic reasoning becomes a circular argument for those who strongly believe in evolution, since they try to fit all their scientific findings into their worldview while excluding what doesn't fit, including, of course, stories from the Bible. See John

Lennox's book *God's Undertaker: Has Science Buried God?*[2] in which he presents a strong case for God as the intelligent, powerful Creator of the universe.

Today we have an increasing number of people who would believe in the Lord Jesus for their salvation but deny the miracle of creation as given to us in Scripture or that we human beings are uniquely made in God's image. They no longer believe evil in the world came because of the disobedience of Adam and Eve or even that God already judged the world once in a worldwide cataclysm of watery destruction and will do so again—and this time by fire. But consider these sobering verses by the apostle Peter in his second epistle.

> They will say, "Where is the promise of his coming? For ever since the fathers fell asleep, all things are continuing as they were from the beginning of creation [uniformitarianism]." For they deliberately overlook this fact, that the heavens existed long ago, and the earth was formed out of water and through water by the word of God, and that by means of these the world that then existed was deluged with water and perished. But by the same word the heavens and earth that now exist are stored up for fire, being kept until the day of judgment and destruction of the ungodly.
>
> But do not overlook this one fact, beloved, that with the Lord one day is as a thousand years, and a thousand years as one day. The Lord is not slow to fulfill his promise as some count slowness, but is patient toward you, not wishing that any should perish, but that all should reach repentance. But the day of the Lord will come like a thief, and then the heavens will pass away with a roar, and the heavenly bodies will be burned up and dissolved, and the earth and the works that are done on it will be exposed.
>
> Since all these things are thus to be dissolved, what sort of people ought you to be. (2 Peter 3:4–11)

We can scarcely comprehend the destruction that already occurred in that first judgment much less imagine the one that's to come, but we should try. Peter says here that even in his day people were denying the flood judgment. But believing God's Word that it did occur should affect the way we live our lives, especially considering what's coming next.

Going back to origins, it is necessary, if we believe in the theory of evolution, to make room for it by assigning millions of years to the age of the rocks. Evolution occurring through purposeless, random genetic events takes a long time! But this timeline is simply imposed arbitrarily in an attempt to align what we observe with evolutionary theory. Without this necessity and by believing the Scripture that the earth does have a catastrophic past, a much younger age compared to the earth can be readily seen in the geological formations and the lack of sedimentary buildup between the layers of rock. The implications of believing in evolution as an explanation of origins are vast, including undermining the veracity of Scripture, the omniscience of God, the reality and origin of sin, and humanity's need and hope for salvation.

I am personally convinced that though there is conflict between the prevailing scientific worldview of naturalism and the Christian faith, there is none between real science and faith. Over the last several centuries, in fact, men of faith were those who made the greatest strides in our understanding of the workings of the natural world God has made. Then in mid-1800s, there was an almost-frenzied excitement among the agnostic elites in the scientific world when Darwin proposed a theory called "evolution through natural selection." This theory claimed to do away with the need for God to account for life and its origin. Despite no proof coming forward of finding genuinely new and useful genetic information able to be produced by this mechanism in any organism over the past 150 years and the complete lack of an evolutionary explanation for the origin of life, it has been aggressively taught as fact in schools. Certainly, we can see the amazing diversity of life as living creatures are able to adapt to changes in their environment through built-in genetic adaptability and sometimes even the loss of genetic information, rather than occurring from the acquiring of genuinely new genetic information through random mutation.

More recently, however, the complexity of the DNA language and the information codes built into even the simplest organism have made this theory of evolution increasingly tenuous and statistically impossible. The information required to manufacture and maintain life in any living organism is enormous and required to be there at its very beginning. It is only now that this is being more fully understood.

The power of Satan to seduce us with new scientific discoveries today and the rebellious nature in our hearts against God, which would respond to that, have together led us away from our Creator and his truth and toward what is essentially a worship of this scientific naturalism. Scripture tells us that anything worshipped other than God becomes an idol. See what the apostle John says. "We know that we [speaking to believers in Christ] are from God, and the whole world lies in the power of the evil one. And we know that the Son of God has come and has given us understanding, so that we may know him who is true; and we are in him who is true, in his Son Jesus Christ. He is the true God and eternal life. Little children, keep yourselves from idols" (1 John 5:19–21).

So for many, evolution has now become that idol. The phrase in the first line above, that "the whole world lies in the power of the evil one," meaning of Satan, ought to jolt us awake to the reality of life in this world in which we live. That's why Paul tells us about the necessity of the Christian armor in Ephesians 6. From time to time, one of Satan's flaming darts will find its mark in us. It's inevitable, and we must be ready to stand against him. The antidote is faith in God and a knowledge of and confidence in his Word. So let us undertake to read it, becoming conversant with its truth and strengthened in our faith as we live behind enemy lines in this world where Satan calls himself god.

Where then do we go from here in finding our way through what may at times appear to be an endless maze? Where can we find something reliable to trust, something to give us lasting peace? It seems that for the most part, all these problems arise because of a failure to understand the essential character of God and then not to see the verses of Scripture within their specific contexts by careful examination of his Word. We must always ask, "What is the purpose of the paragraph within which this particular text appears?" The Bible, as the unchanging and inspired eternal Word of the living God, is harmonious and coherent within itself and will never contradict either itself or the character of God it reveals.

In this short treatise then, I have tried to be *homo unius libri* (a man of one book), which some will, I'm sure, criticize for being too narrow. But the Bible is God's book, the eternal, unchanging inspired Word of God, and it should suffice and be authoritative in our lives as we read it and do careful study of its message (Matthew 5:17–18; 2 Timothy 3:16; 2 Peter 1:19–21). In addition, I have tried to consciously steer away from making this into an academic exercise.

Most importantly, let us always remember that salvation is most critically to be found not primarily in a philosophy or even in a theology but in a person. The apostle Peter, when brought before the Sanhedrin to justify the message being preached, said, "This Jesus is the stone that was rejected by you, the builders, which has become the cornerstone. And *there is salvation in no one else*, for there is no other name under heaven given among men by which we must be saved" (Acts 4:11–12, emphasis added).

The apostle John certainly believed this as well and wrote extensively in his Gospel to confirm this foundational truth. He started right in chapter 1 with these first verses of affirmation of our Lord's deity and his incarnation and the grace and truth that came to us through him. "In the beginning was the Word, and the Word was with God, and the Word was God ... And the Word became flesh and dwelt among us, and we have seen his glory, glory as of the only Son from the Father, full of grace and truth ... grace and truth came through Jesus Christ" (John 1:1, 14, 17).

Finally, in John's Gospel, the Lord Jesus tells Peter and then also John to "follow me" (John 21:19). And that's what we must do as well— follow him and not cleverly devised systems of men. We must follow him through a careful study of his Word and a willingness to respond to the truths revealed in grateful obedience.

In doing this study, I have shone the light of Scripture into some dusty corners of our theological beliefs and customs. Certainly, I have been critical of some belief systems and certain interpretations of Scripture, but recognizing the oneness of the body of Christ, which is loved by God, I don't wish to be critical or put down any particular fellow traveler. Also, this paper is certainly not written just for the academic student, but I trust it will be taken in the context in which it was written as an impetus for further study for all believers to give clarity and assurance that our roots are firmly anchored in the soil of God's eternal Word.

Introduction

◈ THE PREMISES

Several foundational biblical premises underlie the importance of considering this subject of salvation. First is the understanding that there is an eternal, sovereign God, who is our Creator and to whom we all, human beings, must give an account (1 Peter 4:5), so getting it right is important. See what the following verses tell us, first in Genesis. "In the beginning God created the heavens and the earth." And further, Moses wrote in Genesis 1, "So God created man in his own image, in the image of God he created him; male and female he created them. And God blessed them" (Genesis 1:27–28).

As well both Romans and Hebrews tell us of our ultimate responsibility to God for how we use the life we've been given.

> For it is written, "As I live, says the Lord, every knee shall bow to me, and every tongue shall confess to God." So then each of us will give an account of himself to God. (Romans 14:11–12)

> No creature is hidden from his sight, but all are naked and exposed to the eyes of him *to whom we must give account.* (Hebrews 4:13 emphasis added)

It's important to notice that the Bible, God's book, doesn't try to prove his existence except to say his existence is self-evident (Romans

1:18–20) and that only a fool would disbelieve this core understanding of reality (Psalm 10:3–4; 14:1–3).

The second premise is that God created life and in particular mankind as a special creation, made in his image, with an eternal spirit, moral awareness, and an ability to freely choose our way. Even Darwin recognized that going from inorganic material to life was an evolutionary mystery. Going the next step from life to human life is an even greater leap as much as naturalistic scientists would like to call us simply the most evolved species. And as we learn more about the complexities of life, the impossibility of it is even more evident today. God made us and did so that he might show his love to us and have joy in seeing us love others and himself in return.

The third premise isn't a happy truth, but it is that as human beings, we are fallen creatures, separated from our God because of having disobeyed and chosen our own way, starting in the Garden of Eden and consequently resulting in now having within us a sin nature (Romans 5:16–20). We see the story of our original parents and their decision to disobey their Maker in Genesis 3. There is nothing in this account to suggest the telling of a mere myth but rather a factual reporting of what transpired on that fateful day. Now stuck in this dire predicament as sinners and living within Satan's domain yet still desiring reconciliation with God, we need help. Indeed, we are in desperate need, since that day in the garden until now, of help for salvation and divine intervention.

With Satan's encouragement, there have been many attempts made by human beings to find our own way back to God, such as Hinduism, Buddhism, Islam, or several thousand other religions, all focused on us doing something, on our futile works to make one righteousness.

The fourth premise is that God has provided this salvation for us, a way back to him, through the provision and sacrifice of his Son at Calvary. This is the subject and focus of this paper. The curious thing for Christians is why, when we have God's unchanging Word to give us the answers, there should also be so many different understandings about this salvation God offers to us, this singular way of reconnecting with him. But Satan has worked diligently and often successfully to confuse us and obscure the way. Then there is our own fallen human nature, which desperately wants to have some part in it; there must be something we must or can do to facilitate this reconciliation. Then there are others, who, while trying to correct this problem of the "flesh," have overcorrected to the point of, in their theology, impugning the very character of God with a fatalistic view of who will and won't be saved.

Lastly, the fifth premise is that the Bible is God's inerrant, infallible revelation of his wisdom and will to us. It is a book that cannot become outdated but instead gives us an understanding of God—who he is, his intrinsic unchanging character, and his eternal plans for us, his people. Jesus frequently referred to the Scripture in his messages, saying, "For truly, I say to you, until heaven and earth pass away, not an iota, not a dot, will pass from the Law until all is accomplished" (Matthew 5:18–19). And then again: "Heaven and earth will pass away, but my words will not pass away" (Matthew 24:35). So we can be confident of its truth, knowing it is a guide for us through this life as we seek to follow him and do his will.

✦ STARTING AT THE BEGINNING

> Then the Lord God said, "Behold, the man has become like one of us in knowing good and evil. Now, lest he reach out his hand and take also of the tree of life and eat and live forever—" therefore the Lord God sent him out from the garden of Eden to work the ground from which he was taken. He drove out the man, and at the east of the garden of Eden he placed the cherubim and a flaming sword that turned every way to guard the way to the tree of life. (Genesis 3:22–24)

What a vivid and tragic picture as we see Adam and Eve being driven out of the Garden of Eden, driven out from all they had ever known because of their disobedience and now-fallen state! Despite the severity of this action, there was yet a kindness involved. As God says, his concern was that if left there, they might eat of the fruit of the tree of life and live forever, inferring that it would then leave them in a permanent, sinful state.

Let's be clear. This story Moses recorded about our first parents is, as said above, not a myth but written history, as the style of writing and specific details would indicate. God created them, the first human beings, perfect and in his image. Unlike the myth of evolution, mankind didn't arise from the muck and gradually develop sentience and speech; they were as human beings able from the beginning to walk and talk with the Lord. That's why it's always surprising to secular archaeologists when they uncover a very old civilization that seems so "advanced" and that doesn't fit into their worldview. But it was from this first perfect state that they fell. Eve was deceived by Satan, who is also real, and she gave the forbidden fruit to Adam, who was with her and chose to follow Eve in believing Satan's lies and disobeying God. Instantly they died spiritually, cut off from their relationship with God (Genesis 3:1–13).

Ever since then, all mankind has been born in this state of alienation from God with a natural inclination to self-centeredness and rebellion against their Creator. Scripture calls this our "fallen" state (Psalm 53:3), and truly nothing else can account so well for the existence of evil in the world. All would agree, no doubt, that evil really does exist, even the evolutionists. Yet logically they would say that all human behavior is caused by the built-in drive to propagate our genes, which leaves no room for even the concept of evil. Yet coming to Scripture, we see how it accounts for our complete inability to consistently do good. By inference, of course, if this story is a myth and we don't have a sin nature, we don't need salvation, so Jesus didn't need to die for us. Therefore, the whole of the New Testament is essentially useless. But let's be real; we do sin, all of us, and our Savior did die—and thank God for that!

Less than two millennia after this rebellion in the garden, we read these awful words. "The Lord saw that the wickedness of man was great in the earth, and that every intention of the thoughts of his heart was only evil continually. And the Lord was sorry that he had made man on the earth, and it grieved him to his heart. So the Lord said, 'I will blot out man whom I have created from the face of the land'" (Genesis 6:5–7).

Consequently, God sent the world-destroying flood, and humanity started anew with just Noah and his family. To call this event "Noah's Flood" greatly minimizes what really occurred. This wasn't just some extra-heavy localized rainstorm but a worldwide cataclysm and flooding of whole continents, associated with the rapid moving apart of the tectonic plates, the very foundations of the earth, as shown clearly in the geological record. But despite the cleansing of the earth, people remained hopelessly lost. We still needed a Savior.

Humanity has never recovered from the forced separation that occurred in the garden following our sin of disobedience since as human beings we had been created for the very purpose of enjoying fellowship with God. And though we now no longer are fit for his presence, we long for it still. So, from Scripture, we can see that the need for salvation started right in the garden.

Repeatedly in Scripture when cherubim are mentioned, we see them as these great celestial beings of heavenly origin guarding the holiness and glory of God. And we first see them here protecting the entrance to the Garden of Eden and the tree of life within. "He drove out the man, and at the east of the garden of Eden he placed the cherubim and a flaming sword that turned every way to guard the way to the tree of life" (Genesis 3:24).

Again, we see them represented by the two golden cherubim statues in the tabernacle above the mercy seat, where they were bending over, symbolically looking down into the ark, where they would see the words of the Law. To mitigate the required judgment on the people because of having acted against God's holiness and broken this law, it was necessary for the high priest to sprinkle blood from the goat of the sin offering on the mercy seat so the law could then be seen by the cherubim figuratively *through the atoning blood*, and God could be merciful to his people. This yearly ritual was an act of "atonement"—meaning to cover or appease. See how Paul explains this when he writes, "In his divine forbearance, [God] passed over former sins" (Romans 3:25). So full payment wasn't able to be paid at that time through animal sacrifice, but in his mercy, God for a time was satisfied with Israel's acknowledgment of their sin and their approach to him for mercy in this way.

Down through the ages, people have felt this estrangement, this distance, between themselves and God because of his holiness and our sin. What could bridge this great gap? As the centuries and ages have passed, we see all the many manmade, Satan-inspired religions (approximately forty-three hundred to date, according to Google.ca) being created to give men something to do or someone to worship to fill this void, this God-given need.

God, however, because of his love from the very beginning provided a way for us human beings to approach him, even in our sin and despite his holiness. But there was a right way and a wrong way to do so consistent with God's holy character, and consequences were involved in choosing that way, as Cain and Abel discovered. Entering God's presence must be done as an act of faith in acknowledging him as holy and yet One who still desires us, though we are sinners, to come before him. It must, second, be done with an acknowledgment of the seriousness of sinning against God. The punishment was to be the death of the sinner. But God provided that a substitute could be used and its blood shed as a symbol of this death. So while no works of ours would suffice, forgiveness must involve a blood sacrifice, as we're told in Hebrews. "Without the shedding of blood there is no forgiveness of sins" (Hebrews 9:22).

Unfortunately, our sinful nature and resultant self-centeredness and pride push us to try to fix the problem on our own terms or to come in our own way, as Cain tried to do. At other times people have decided to set their sights on some lesser god, possibly seen as more accessible and not so demanding and allowing them to contribute to the renewal of this spiritual relationship.

Coming to the New Testament, we read the amazing story of the incarnation as God the Son became a human being, called the "second man" or the last Adam, and at Calvary he shed his blood and died for us. Then on the third day, he rose in triumph from the dead, having paid the penalty and broken the power of sin. No human being on his own could ever accomplish this work of forgiveness of sins, not only because of the sin nature within us but because of the limitations of our humanity. It took incarnate deity to rescue us yet someone who could act as a mediator, who could identify with both mortal man and eternal God to bridge the great gap between us. This is what Paul wrote to Timothy when he said, "There is one God, and there is one mediator between God and men, the man Christ Jesus, who gave himself as a ransom for all" (1 Timothy 2:5–6).

It took this unique entity, the God-man (the hypostasis of two natures within one person) to accomplish what no one else could. As a man, he died for us and opened for us a new and permanent way of access to God. Sadly, many falsely claiming to be Christians or others, sincere but misled believers, have-twisted the simplicity of this good news, adding works to a completed work or saying there is some higher plane of spirituality we must, after trusting in Christ, still strive toward to complete our salvation. Or their system of belief is such that it keeps people in fear of losing their salvation. Of course, this is an activity of Satan as he tries to keep people from the truth and the peace that comes from trusting in Christ for the eternal salvation he provides. And it is Satan who continues to make stumble those who have found this salvation by depriving them of the certainty of it and the peace we are promised.

So today, despite the gospel message truly being such good news, there are many differences of opinion and much confusion about how a person can be reconciled to God. Some, especially in Eastern religions, pessimistically believe it's an impossible goal and instead focus on finding escape from the endless sufferings of this life as they strive to lose their identity and individuality by becoming one with the universe. They call this "nirvana," but it is truly no paradise to settle for being satisfied to find peace by ceasing to exist as individuals. What a life goal! The Christian faith in its simplicity is so much more than that, yet even here there have been many attempts to twist it. We will look at a number of these in this paper.

✦ THE QUESTIONS PROPOSED

Here are some of the concerns, questions, and controversies I have heard and examined within the sphere of the Christian faith over the years and that pushed me into this study:

- Was Christ's death at Calvary sufficient to pay the price for the salvation of all people, for all their sins, and for all time?
- That being the case, in the end, will God in his love just save everyone anyway (sometimes called "universalism")?

- What about those who have never heard the gospel? Will they all perish?
- Can we or must we contribute to our salvation? Did Calvary just open the door, which we must then walk through by our own effort?
- Can all come and be saved? Has God made salvation available for everyone?
- Does God need to regenerate a person first before he or she can then necessarily believe? Said another way, is a person so spiritually dead that he or she has lost the God-given ability of free will to choose or reject the offer of salvation?
- How is a person saved today?
- If a person chooses Christ, can he or she later choose not to believe, walk away from the faith, and be lost?
- Are there two parts to this salvation—accepting Jesus as Savior and then, second, needing to accept him as Lord to truly be saved?
- A slightly different question would be this: are there two parts to salvation—accepting Jesus as Savior and later inviting the Holy Spirit to indwell and empower us?
- Must we come to the point of complete resignation of our lostness before God can supernaturally open our eyes to the gift of his salvation?
- How can we know for sure we are eternally saved?
- What if we struggle with our assurance? Does that mean we aren't really saved?
- Is baptism a necessary part of this salvation?

Before specifically dealing with these questions, we must first explore the many theological terms in Scripture associated with salvation that help us see its many different aspects. These are words like *justification, redemption, reconciliation, regeneration, substitution, the new birth, sanctification,* and *eternal security.* Still other associated words to look at include *grace, faith, conviction, repentance, propitiation,* and *forgiveness.* Do each of these concepts have a place and part in our salvation? If so, where does each fit in, and is there some order involved? In addition, how does each contribute to the picture as a whole? So, first, we'll look at the meaning of these important words as used in Scripture and how they each contribute to our understanding of what the Bible calls this "so great salvation" (Hebrews 2:3).

To do this, we first need to be prepared to believe that the Scriptures are the unchanging, eternal, and inspired words of God, a revelation of himself and his plans for us; therefore, they are wholly true and authoritative to us as they were when first given and as Scripture itself affirms. Then we must go to these Scriptures and do careful exegesis of these key words as used in their context. It will be necessary to take great care to avoid the pitfalls of adhering to systems of theology supported by one group or another, since these tend to create confusion and can certainly lead us away from the truth as given in the inspired Word of God.

In going about this study, we ought to do several things. First, we need to define the terms from Scripture, looking for the places they are found and how they are used in their context.

Second, we should look for actual salvation stories in the Bible. These will be patterns for us.

Third, it is important to look for biblical passages that give us the theology on the subject, a summary of God's thoughts on the matter.

Then it will be instructive to propose an order to the events associated with our salvation, realizing that some occur simultaneously with others and that many Christian denominations have put these events in a very different order.

Lastly, understanding who is involved will be central to our study since this salvation must take into consideration both the complete nature and character of God, who planned it, and the essence of human beings, whom God created and planned to be its recipients.

Chapter One

A Word Study of Biblical Salvation Terms

Each of these sections will start with a word picture and a passage of Scripture that gives us the essence of the word under investigation.

❖ **SALVATION**

> Save me, O God!
> For the waters have come up to my neck.
> I sink in deep mire,
> where there is no foothold;
> I have come into deep waters,
> and the flood sweeps over me.
> —Psalm 69:1–2

David cries out to God in this messianic psalm with a graphic word picture of someone about to drown with no solid footing and with none to help. How like the sinner needing God's saving intervention this is!

In the Old Testament, the premier picture of salvation is found by looking at Jesus's namesake, Joshua (Joshua 1). This first commander of the army of Israel did as the Lord commanded and with strength and courage led God's people victoriously into the land of Canaan. What a fitting picture of the deliverance and victory now provided to us through our Lord Jesus Christ! And what a great length our Savior was willing to go for us! "Since therefore the children share in flesh and blood, he himself likewise partook of the same things, that through death he might destroy the one who has the power of death, that is, the devil, and *deliver* [save, release, or set free] all those who through fear of death were subject to lifelong slavery" (Hebrews 2:14–15, emphasis added).

So what are we talking about when we use the word *salvation*? When I was growing up, I often heard the phrase that so-and-so "got saved" last night," which is a rather poor use of substituting a verb where a noun was needed. But we all knew what was meant—someone had taken the important, life-changing step of trusting the Lord Jesus Christ as his or her Savior.

If we look up the word in a dictionary, it tells us salvation is "the act of rescuing or protecting someone from harm, risk, loss, destruction" or "the state of having been taken out of or protected from harm, risk, etc."[3]

In Scripture, the word *salvation* in Hebrew (*yesu 'ah*) appears about seventy-eight times in the Old Testament and refers primarily to God's acts of help, mainly to the children of Israel; these have already occurred and been experienced, connected to the concept of being set free. Then in Matthew 1:21, God tells Joseph that the child Mary was to bear is to be called Jesus, "for he will save his people from their sins" (Matthew 1:21). This name is mentioned 965 times in the New Testament. The original word in Hebrew is the same as the Old Testament name Joshua (*Yehowshu'a*) and means "Jehovah will save." Jewish believers today still refer to Jesus by the contraction *Yeshua*.

Going back even earlier, before Joshua, we are told the amazing story in the book of Exodus about how Jehovah God delivered the children of Israel, who were slaves in Egypt. We read of the miracles of the ten plagues culminating in the death of all the firstborn in the houses not covered by the blood of a lamb. The people were helplessly enslaved, and God saved them and victoriously brought them out to follow Moses to the Promised Land.

Coming now to the New Testament, the Greek word for salvation is *soterio*, which denotes preservation, deliverance from danger or capture, or, as more precisely defined by W. E. Vine, "the spiritual and eternal deliverance granted immediately by God to those who accept His conditions of repentance and faith in the Lord Jesus, in whom alone it is to be obtained."[4] It occurs in both the noun and verb forms 137 times in the New Testament. The study of salvation is therefore more formally called "soteriology."

Let's look at this word in its context as Luke recounts Peter's defense before the Sanhedrin after the disciples were arrested in Jerusalem for preaching this message of salvation after healing a crippled man.

> Then Peter, filled with the Holy Spirit, said to them, "Rulers of the people and elders, if we are being examined today concerning a good deed done to a crippled man, by what means this man has been healed, let it be known to all of you and to all the people of Israel that by the name of Jesus Christ of Nazareth, whom you crucified, whom God raised from the dead—by him this man is standing before you well. This Jesus is the stone that was rejected by you, the builders, which has become the cornerstone. And *there is salvation in no one else*, for there is no other name under heaven given among men by which we must be saved." (Acts 4:8–12, emphasis added)

First, he summarizes the message. Jesus was the Messiah sent from heaven. After being rejected by the Jews, he was crucified but then in triumph rose from the dead as the Savior of sinners.

Peter attests to the exclusivity of this message—a salvation available through no other means or persons but Jesus alone. This message remains unchanged today. Jesus is the way, and only in him do we find forgiveness of sin and life everlasting.

When we look at the New Testament, we find that the message of salvation is called "the gospel" or "the good news." This word *gospel* is derived from the old Anglo-Saxon term *god-spell*, meaning good story, a rendering of the Latin *evangelium* and the Greek *euangelion*, meaning "good news" or "good telling."

This word *gospel*, speaking of the message of salvation, is used ninety-six times in the New Testament. In fact, this is without a doubt one of the main themes in the New Testament. Going back to the word *salvation*, we see that in its general usage it's a word that can be used in a number of different contexts. One could be describing a daring rescue that saved someone from certain death in a particular situation or alternatively, spiritual rebirth.

Several years ago, I had a very old patient, a man who had served as a soldier in Europe during World War II. Rae had a shadow box on the wall of his room in the long-term care facility where he resided. In it were various medals and mementos honoring his participation in the war. One appeared somewhat out of place compared to the others. It was a small, damaged Gideon New Testament. I heard the story from another person of how one day, during an offensive, Rae had been saved by that New Testament in his left breast pocket. He was hit by a bullet that penetrated about three-quarters of the way through the small Bible before being stopped. The book saved his life. Whether he had ever read it sufficiently that it gave him eternal salvation, I don't know. But its words had the power to save his soul just as the paper pages that day saved him physically.

There are many alternative words and expressions in the Scriptures for this word *salvation* that will add to our understanding, but the most important thing to find out is, from a biblical context, from what we are or will be saved or rescued. We read these life-giving words penned by the apostle John: "For God so loved the world, that he gave his only Son, that *whoever believes in him should not perish* but have eternal life [salvation]" (John 3:16, emphasis added).

This tells us that without believing or trusting in Jesus, the opposite of being saved will happen. We will perish, being forever separated from God and from the possibility of salvation, and this is because, as verse 18 says, we are "condemned already." As a result, as we see at the end of this chapter, "whoever believes in the Son has eternal life; whoever does not obey the Son shall not see life, but *the wrath of God remains on him*" (John 3:36, emphasis added).

God's wrath remains on us, and it's because of our sins. What a heavy load to bear! As human beings made in his image, even though we are marred by sin and in rebellion against him, he loves us still; yet as freewill beings, we remain responsible for our actions and the results of our choices. In his holiness, God hates our sin. Sin means to act or even to think in ways that are against God's perfect will and character. It is to live in independence and rebellion from him. And it must be punished. Yet if we desire to hold on to our sin and live our lives in that state, in our sin nature, then that wrath will continue to rest on us.

In using this word *salvation*, we are talking about being saved from the consequences of the sin that separates us from God. It is that sin that makes us guilty before him and condemns us to being eternally lost. What we then desperately need is to be forgiven of our sin. Most importantly, we see that this salvation is both *needed by all* because of God's holiness (Paul says, "All have sinned and fall short of the glory of God" [Romans 3:23]) and *available to all* because of God's love. Peter says, "Not wishing that any should perish, but that all should reach repentance" (2 Peter 3:9). But it must be received individually by each person, as the invitation John gave says. "The Spirit and the Bride say, 'Come.] And let the one who hears say, 'Come.' And let the one who is thirsty come; let the one who desires take the water of life without price" (Revelation 22:17).

Let's go back to the very beginning and look at the story of the first couple God created. Adam and Eve were in the idyllic Garden of Eden and were enjoying a relationship with God, their Creator, who would come down to them as a theophany that they might enjoy his company or fellowship. A theophany is an appearance by God, no doubt God the Son, taking on the form of a human being to interact with them. What wonderful times they must have had together! Then came the day when they listened to the serpent (Satan in disguise) and disobeyed the one restriction God had placed on them. Immediately, with that act of rebellion, they felt naked and ashamed and for the first time experienced guilt triggered by that moral code God had placed within them. The age of innocence was over, and that close relationship with their Creator was immediately severed. In other words, it brought about within them a state the Bible speaks of as "spiritual death." "And you were dead in the trespasses and sins in which you once walked, following the course of this world, following the prince of the power of the air, the spirit that is now at work in the sons of disobedience" (Ephesians 2:1–3).

Being separated from a holy God (called "spiritual death") also eventually led to their physical death as well because of the sin nature now within them. Paul clarifies this for us by saying, "Therefore, just as sin came into the world through one man, and death through sin, and so death spread to all men because all sinned" (Romans 5:12). Yet the echo of that lost relationship continues to resonate within the heart of each of us to this very day.

On the positive side, post fall and now also post Calvary, the good news of the gospel tells us that those who have trusted in Christ have been saved, meaning given eternal life and been made spiritually alive. This includes being brought back into a relationship with God (see also the section on reconciliation later in this chapter). With that also comes his sure promise of fellowship with him during this life and eventually, but most certainly, being brought to a state when the sin nature within will be fully gone and when we will be made completely holy and blameless before him. No doubt this will occur shortly after his return to the air to call us up to himself. We can read what Paul wrote concerning the rapture in his first letter to the Corinthians. "Behold! I tell you a mystery. We shall not all sleep, but we shall all be changed, in a moment, in the twinkling of an eye, at the last trumpet. For the trumpet will sound, and the dead will be raised imperishable, and *we shall be changed*" (1 Corinthians 15:51–52, emphasis added).

Salvation is something not just to be believed as a doctrine but something to be lived. And it is so much more than one word can possibly explain, so the next sections describe some of the many facets of this wonderful gift God has provided and desires for us—to change us inside and out.

◆ REDEMPTION

> O Israel, hope in the Lord!
> For with the Lord there is steadfast love,
> and with him is plentiful redemption.
> And he will redeem Israel
> from all his iniquities.
> —Psalm 130:7–8

Sin is both an attitude and resulting rebellious actions against God. God sees righting this in this passage in terms of a debt that requires payment. "Be on guard for yourselves and for all the flock, among which the Holy Spirit has made you overseers, to shepherd the church of God *which He purchased with His own blood*" (Acts 20:28–29 NASB, emphasis added).

I'd like to start this section by retelling a story I heard as a boy about another small boy and his boat.

> There was a boy who had painstakingly built a model sailboat. He was very proud of what he had built, so when it was finally completed, he decided that he would test it out on the open water.
>
> Then he excitedly placed the boat in the water. He gave it a gentle push, and it took off. The wind caught the sails. The boat cut through the water much better than expected. What a sight!
>
> But then, unexpectedly, before the boy realized what was happening, the sailboat just kept going rapidly into the distance. The boy quickly waded into the water with the hope of catching up to it, but it had gone out too far. The boat faded off into the distance … and disappeared. It was gone.
>
> Sometime later, the boy was walking downtown and passed a second-hand store. There in the window, he saw the sailboat he had labored to build. He went into the store and went up to the sailboat. Some of the paint

had worn off, but he'd have known the boat anywhere. He picked it up and said to the store owner, "This boat is mine!" He held it in his arms and began to walk out of the store.

The owner, of course, said, "Wait a minute now. It's my boat! I paid someone for it."

The boy said, "No, no, no. It's *my* boat. I made it! Look at the little scratches I did … Here are my initials on the bottom."

But the owner said, "I'm sorry, sonny. If you want it, you're going to have to pay for it."

The poor little guy went home to see what odd jobs he could do to earn enough money to purchase the sailboat back.

Finally, one day, he had enough money. The boy went back to the store and bought back his boat. As he left the store, holding the sailboat close to his chest, the boy could be heard saying, "You're my boat. You're twice my boat. First, because I made you and now because I bought you."[5]

What a great story illustration for this word *redemption*! It reminds us of our being initially created by God but then of the need, because we are now lost, for him to repurchase us at Calvary.

"*Christ redeemed us* from the curse of the law by becoming a curse for us—for it is written, 'Cursed is everyone who is hanged on a tree'—so that in Christ Jesus the blessing of Abraham might come to the Gentiles, so that we might receive the promised Spirit through faith" (Galatians 3:13–14, emphasis added).

The word *redemption* (Greek, *lutrosis*), along with its alternate verb forms, *redeem* and *ransom*, occurs about sixteen times in the New Testament. It reminds us that a price needed to be paid for our salvation since our sins were an offense to a holy God, separating us from him.

Today we sometimes hear of captives taken by a terrorist organization and a ransom being required to free them. What would it take to free us from the bondage of sin and Satan? Scripture gives us the answer. "Knowing that you were ransomed from the futile ways inherited from your forefathers, not with perishable things such as silver or gold, but with *the precious blood of Christ*" (1 Peter 18–19, emphasis added).

It's important to see that though before our salvation and as sinners we were enslaved to Satan, the god of this world, yet it is not to him that the ransom is paid but to our original Maker, the Creator God. Now as to the verse above, the word *precious* here has the meaning of something of great value, something costly. Here we are told that it's the blood of Christ that is precious, representative of his life. In the Old Testament, the Law called for a life for a life, the *lex talionis*. But here it's not just another human life being spoken of. It's the life of the Son of Man, God manifest in the flesh. Peter was right; it is of infinite value. The ransom, then, is sufficient in God's eyes (Romans 3:25; 1 John 4:10) and can be applied to all who trust Jesus as Savior.

Yes, the price was high—the death of the sinless man, Christ Jesus, on the cross at Calvary—but it was done that he might not only remove our condemnation but also make us holy before him. Paul uses this word in writing to Titus about the Lord when he says, "*Who gave himself for us to redeem [or ransom] us from all lawlessness* and to purify for himself a people for his own possession who are zealous for good works" (Titus 2:14). He redeemed us and has begun in us a work of purification to make us holy before him.

Another word that is close in meaning and comes from the Old Testament is *atonement*. Here the meaning was "to pacify" the one offended or "to cover," suggesting something more temporary in nature, like a down payment. And indeed, these sacrifices of animals were required over and over again, picturing and awaiting their final fulfillment in Christ. In the New Testament, the word *atonement* is generally translated "sacrifice." The joy spoken of in the old gospel song by Fanny Crosby is so true when it says,

> Redeemed how I love to proclaim it, redeemed by the blood of the Lamb.
> Redeemed by his infinite mercy, His child and forever I am.

The songwriter's joy is very evidently focused on the price that was paid for her salvation and the extent of it. And that's the meaning of this word *redeemed*, which means not only to buy something but also to buy it back, implying a previous right of ownership. Fanny Crosby's thoughts are here focused on the infinite value of Jesus's blood given up to the Father in heaven on our behalf. And as another songwriter, Andraé Crouch, wrote, "The blood ... will never lose its power." He had taken this truth directly from the words of the writer of Hebrews, who clarifies it for us by saying, "But when Christ had offered for all time a single sacrifice for sins, he sat down at the right hand of God, waiting from that time until his enemies should be made a footstool for his feet. For by a single offering, he has perfected for all time those who are being sanctified" (Hebrews 10:12–14).

And, unlike the priests of old, Jesus will live forever to make intercession for us, as the writer of Hebrews says. "Consequently, he is able to save to the uttermost those who draw near to God through him, since he always lives to make intercession for them" (Hebrews 7:25). How wonderful that his shed blood paid the steep price for a salvation we could never pay, and he is now able to save "to the uttermost," declaring salvation open to everyone and for all time.

＊ JUSTIFICATION

> God looks down from heaven
> on the children of man
> to see if there are any who understand,
> who seek after God.
>
> They have all fallen away;
> together they have become corrupt;
> there is none who does good,
> not even one.
> —Psalm 53:2–3

The picture that comes to mind here is the amazing occurrence in ancient times of Abraham arguing his case before the Lord for the deliverance of his nephew Lot from God's destruction about to fall on Sodom because of their sin. He was reminding God, of all things, that in his very nature God is just when he said, "Shall not the Judge of all the earth do what is just?" (Genesis 18:25–26). So that being true, how could he not save Abraham's nephew Lot and any other righteous people within the city? He was no doubt thinking of Lot's family and their spouses and children, but it appears they had been absorbed in the paganism and sin of the city.

Today an even harder question can be asked: How can our unchanging Creator God be just and yet at the same time be the One who "justifies the ungodly" (Romans 4:5)? See how Paul explains this apparent paradox in Romans 3.

> For there is no distinction: for all have sinned and fall short of the glory of God, and are justified by his grace as a gift, through the redemption that is in Christ Jesus, whom God put forward as a propitiation by his blood, to be received by faith. This was to show God's righteousness, because in his divine forbearance he had passed over former sins. It was to show his righteousness at the present time, so *that he might be just and the justifier of the one who has faith in Jesus.* Then what becomes of our boasting? It is excluded. By what kind of law? By a law of works? No, but by the law of faith. For we hold that *one is justified by faith apart from works of the law.* (Romans 3:22–28, emphasis added)

So here's still another word adding to our understanding of salvation, and it and its various forms occur thirty-six times in the New Testament. The noun in Greek, *dikaiosis*, denotes the action of "declaring someone as righteous or innocent or guiltless," and the verb form *justify* means to absolve or acquit. This passage tells us it's because of the crucifixion of Jesus that God can, by their faith in him, justify the unrighteous. How great then must have been the work done at Calvary to assuage even the righteous anger of a holy God!

Paul here especially uses the term *justified* in its legal sense to help us understand how we sinners can be proclaimed righteous by God. Jesus also gives an example by telling a parable in Luke 18:9–14 about two men who went up to the temple to pray, a Pharisee and a tax collector; and everyone knew at that time just how corrupt these tax men were. The Pharisee thanked God for all the good deeds he had done to justify God's favor, but the tax collector, obviously convicted of his wrong deeds and with his head bowed down, just said, "God, be merciful to me, a sinner!" In verse 14, Jesus then concluded the story by saying, "I tell you, *this man* [meaning the tax collector] *went down to his house justified*, rather than the other. For everyone who exalts himself will be humbled, but the one who humbles himself will be exalted" (Luke 18:14, emphasis added).

Before going on, it would be more grammatically correct to translate the tax collector's words as "God be merciful to me *the* sinner," since in the Greek, the definite article is used here. The clear implication of this confession is that this tax collector recognized not only his sin but also the greatness of it as if he were the only sinner in the world. He realized his inability to clear his personal guilt without the intervention of God above. Here we see a heart of contrition coming before God in repentance. It is the opposite of a heart that continues in rebellion against God and it is then with the acknowledgment of guilt, that God's salvation can clear the debt the sinner could never pay. It justifies us today just as surely as it did to him, putting us legally into a right standing before God. No wonder the message is called the "good news"!

Paul explains to us that justification, meaning to obtain a right standing before God or to be made right with God, is possible only by the offering of the blood of Christ. He says, "Since, therefore, we have now been justified *by his blood*, much more shall we be saved by him from the wrath of God" (Romans 5:9, emphasis added). Earlier, Peter proclaimed before the Sanhedrin in Jerusalem, "And there is salvation in no one else, for there is no other name under heaven given among men by which we must be saved" (Acts 4:12). So it can never be through our own so-called works of righteousness. God the Father sees the sacrifice of his Son as the one and only sufficient offering for our sins. This is where the next word in our list comes in.

We must not finish this section without briefly mentioning the related word *forgiveness*. Having been justified before God, we are at the same time forgiven by him. Being declared righteous before God means for us that the slate has been wiped clean (justification), and therefore the pardon has been given (forgiveness). This reminds me of the picture John Bunyan gave of Christian in his book *Pilgrim's Progress*. At that moment when the heavy load slipped from his back, Bunyan wrote, "Then Christian gave three leaps for joy and went on singing."[6] To know God has forgiven us is an amazing thing and must change how we live our lives. The Lord told the disciples to proclaim this message to the nations. "Then he opened their minds to understand the Scriptures, and said to them, 'Thus it is written, that the Christ should suffer and on the third day rise from the dead, and that repentance and forgiveness of sins should be proclaimed in his name to all nations, beginning from Jerusalem'" (Luke 24:45–47).

It's a wonderful thing when another person forgives you. And to be forgiven by God much more so! Isaiah started his book in the Old Testament by calling people to repent and return to God and told them what the result would be: "Come now, let us reason together, says the Lord: though your sins are like scarlet, *they shall be as white as snow*; though they are red like crimson, they shall become like wool" (Isaiah 1:18, emphasis added). Amazingly, God's forgiveness results in the very stain of sin being removed, so then it says in Hebrews, concerning those who are included in the new covenant, "For I will be merciful toward their iniquities, and *I will remember their sins no more*" (Hebrews 8:12, emphasis added).

I remember when I first started working as a physician, occasionally coming home from the office or hospital with bloodstains on my clothes. I wondered whether I'd just have to throw them out. Beth, the office nurse at that time, gave me some white powder to use, and I was amazed! It was an early formulation of an enzyme, and it completely removed the stains. And so it is with us.

God looks on those who have received his salvation as having been permanently cleansed from their sins. The stain of sin is gone, and with it the guilt has been taken away, and we can walk, as it says, "in newness of life" (Romans 6:4).

✦ SUBSTITUTION

> And Abraham lifted up his eyes and looked, and behold,
> behind him was a ram,
> caught in a thicket by his horns.
> And Abraham went and took the ram and offered
> it up as a burnt offering *instead of* his son.
> So, Abraham called the name of that place, "The Lord will provide."
> —Genesis 22:13–14 (emphasis added)

While the word *substitution* isn't found as a noun in the Scriptures, it seems appropriate to be included here because we see word pictures of it in many passages throughout both the Old and New Testaments. The related phrase "instead of" occurs quite frequently in the Old Testament as in Genesis 22 above, where Abraham offered up to God the ram caught in the bushes "instead of" his son, Isaac.

Scripture tells us that in the decrees of our holy God, the punishment of sin is death. Throughout the Old Testament, we see, starting in Genesis 4 with Abel's sacrifice, that God accepted as a temporary measure the death of an animal; it was to be used as a substitute for the person. These pictures were all looking ahead to the coming of the perfect man, who could be our substitute and in dying fully pay for our sin.

> For while we were still weak, at the right time Christ died for the ungodly. For one will scarcely die for a righteous person—though perhaps for a good person one would dare even to die—but God shows his love for us in that while we were still sinners, *Christ died for us*. Since, therefore, we have now been justified by his blood, much more shall we be saved by him from the wrath of God. For if while we were enemies we were reconciled to God by the death of his Son, much more, now that we are reconciled, shall we be saved by his life. (Romans 5:6–10, emphasis added)

Paul says here that in rare instances, someone, his friend, might die for another as his substitute. And we've all no doubt heard wartime stories of men who did this. Posthumously they were honored for their courage and supreme sacrifice. This is what Christ did for us, even though we weren't friends at all but enemies.

Frequently in the Old Testament, we are told about the sacrifices in the Tabernacle, in which a lamb was offered and its blood shed as a substitute for the people. The theological term used is "substitutionary atonement." "When he realizes his guilt in any of these and confesses the sin he has committed, he shall bring to the Lord as his compensation for the sin that he has committed, a female from the flock, a lamb or a goat, for a sin offering. And the priest shall make atonement for him for his sin" (Leviticus 5:5–6).

Also in Genesis 44, we read the story of Judah relating to Joseph (although unknown to him at that time as being his brother) that he had made a pledge of himself to his father Jacob regarding Benjamin's welfare and if necessary, would be a substitute for him.

> Now therefore, as soon as I come to your servant my father, and the boy is not with us, then, as his life is bound up in the boy's life, as soon as he sees that the boy is not with us, he will die, and your servants will bring down the gray hairs of your servant our father with sorrow to Sheol. For your servant became a pledge of safety for the boy to my father, saying, "If I do not bring him back to you, then I shall bear the blame before my father all my life." Now therefore, please let your servant remain *instead of* the boy as a servant to my lord, and let the boy go back with his brothers. (Genesis 44:30–33, emphasis added)

Also, in the New Testament we see many passages referencing this concept, but here are several found just in Hebrews. But first we see the criteria of the substitute: it required the substitute to be not an animal but a man, also one who was perfect, and one, though not subject to death, was able to die for us. In this Jesus not only fully met these requirements but also willingly gave himself. This is more clearly expressed in this passage in Hebrews 10.

> For since the law has but a shadow of the good things to come instead of the true form of these realities, it can never, by the same sacrifices that are continually offered every year, make perfect those who draw near. Otherwise, would they not have ceased to be offered, since the worshipers, having once been cleansed, would no longer have any consciousness of sin? But in these sacrifices, there is a reminder of sin every year. *For it is impossible for the blood of bulls and goats to take away sins* (i.e., to be a fully acceptable substitute). (Hebrew 10:1–4, emphasis added)

Then we also see in Hebrews that this substitutionary sacrifice was to be made by one who was fully human and therefore able to die.

> But we see him who for a little while was made lower than the angels, namely Jesus, crowned with glory and honor because of the suffering of death, so that by the grace of God *he might taste death for everyone* … Since therefore the children share in flesh and blood, he himself likewise partook of the same things, that through death he might destroy the one who has the power of death, that is, the devil, and deliver all those who through fear of death were subject to lifelong slavery. (Hebrews 2:9, 14–15, emphasis added)

Here the text focuses on the necessity of the one offering himself to be a substitute, being able to die and therefore fully satisfy God's righteousness by in fact truly dying in the place of mankind. Paul gives us an oblique reference to the inadequacy of the animal sacrifices as only temporarily covering Israel's sin but not being sufficient to fully substitute for the sins of man. "[Christ Jesus] whom God put forward as a propitiation by his blood, to be received by faith. This was to show

God's righteousness, because *in his divine forbearance he had passed over former sins*" (Romans 3:25, emphasis added).

Finally, we read also in Hebrew, "For it was indeed fitting that we should have such a high priest, holy, innocent, unstained, separated from sinners, and exalted above the heavens. He has no need, like those high priests, to offer sacrifices daily, first for his own sins and then for those of the people, since he did this *once for all* when he offered up himself" (Hebrews 7:26–27, emphasis added).

Jesus was able to be both the priest of God and the offering itself— our perfect substitute. In the Old Testament we see that the main criterion was that the animal be without blemish, yet in all cases, it was an animal's life being given for a person's life. Similarly, in the New Testament, we see the necessity of God the Son becoming human so that as a man he might truly die, pictured as that lamb without blemish, our One and only acceptable substitute, yet as the eternal Son making a sacrifice of eternal benefit. As Peter tells us "For Christ also suffered once for sins, the righteous for the unrighteous, that he might bring us to God, being put to death in the flesh but made alive in the spirit..." (1 Peter 3:18-19)

* ### REGENERATION OR BEING "BORN AGAIN"

> "Jesus answered him, 'Truly, truly, I say to you, unless one is born again, he cannot see the kingdom of God.' Nicodemus said to him, 'How can a man be born when he is old?'" (John 3:3–4).

This biblical principle goes back to the very beginning of time. God spoke to Adam after putting him in the Garden of Eden saying, "You may surely eat of every tree of the garden, but of the tree of the knowledge of good and evil you shall not eat, for in the day that you eat of it you shall surely die" (Genesis 2:16–17). But Adam did partake of the forbidden fruit, following Eve, and immediately spiritual death occurred as they became separated from God, their Creator. Theologically this event is called the "fall" and has been passed on to all people since that fateful day. Paul writes to Titus of the regeneration of man now made available through our Savior. "But when the kindness and love of God our Savior appeared, he saved us, not because of righteous things we had done, but because of his mercy. He saved us through *the washing of rebirth and renewal by the Holy Spirit*" (Titus 3:4–5 NIV, emphasis added).

Many cultures have stories, especially in Egypt, of their belief that the Pharaohs or high-status people would be regenerated after death into gods; therefore, their tombs were packed with all the goods thought necessary for their journey into the afterlife. But in reality none of it was ever used, benefitting no one except the ever-present tomb robbers!

This word *regeneration*, meaning "spiritual rebirth," is found just once, but the phrase "made alive" occurs three times in the epistles. Its use in the New Testament to describe our salvation might seem puzzling, such as when Jesus used it when talking to Nicodemus about his need. Although Nicodemus was a teacher of the Law, Jesus told him, "You must be born again" or regenerated (John 3:7) or given spiritual life.

Remember, humanity was created as living beings both physically alive to the world in which they were created and spiritually alive in their relationship to God. The need for this regeneration or being made alive again takes us right back to the Garden of Eden and Adam's sin. There God had told Adam that he must not eat of the tree of the knowledge of good and evil, "for in the day that you eat of it *you shall surely die*" (Genesis 2:17, emphasis added). In its primary meaning, then, this meant "spiritual death," being separated from God his Creator, the giver of life. And that is exactly what took place that very instant. Paul picks up this metaphor in Ephesians 2:1–2, 4–5, where he says, "And *you were dead* in the trespasses and sins in which you once walked, following the course of this world, following the prince of the power of the air, the spirit that is now at work in the sons of disobedience ... *But God*, being rich in mercy, because of the great love with which he loved us, even when we were dead in our trespasses, *made us alive* [Greek, *sunezooopoíeesen*] together with Christ — by grace you have been saved" (Ephesians 2:1–2, 4–5, emphasis added).

This has the double connotation of being given not only new life but also a life that allows restoration of our relationship with God. Similarly, Paul wrote to the church at Colossae, "And you, *who were dead in your trespasses and the uncircumcision of your flesh, God made alive [regenerated] together with him,* having forgiven us all our trespasses" (Colossians 2:13, emphasis added).

Connected to this idea of regeneration is the apostle John's phrase of being "born again" or born from above, as seen in John 3 (six times) and in 1 John (nine times). This emphasizes the new life that comes with salvation, and being given with this new life in the spirit, as mentioned above, is a restored relationship with God. Nicodemus, though being today's equivalent of the professor of theology in a Christian seminary, was completely confused by this term. He thought only in the literal sense. Finally, Jesus clearly told him that he needed to put his faith in the Son of Man, symbolized by the brass serpent seen in the Old Testament, which Moses lifted up in the wilderness, allowing people to see and believe and be healed of the venomous viper's bite. Likewise in his death, being lifted up on a cross at Calvary, Jesus identified himself with our sin so we might be regenerated and become once again alive unto God. Peter in his first epistle spoke of the source of the power for this regeneration when he said, "According to his great mercy, he has caused us to be born again to a living hope through the resurrection of Jesus Christ from the dead" (1 Peter 1:3).

This power was demonstrated in the resurrection of our Lord Jesus from the dead. He is now able to use this very same power to give us spiritual life. The result is that this new life brings us into a new relationship with God. What an amazing reality!

In addition, with this new life comes the ability to do God's work in the world and to demonstrate the fruit of the Spirit in our lives. Paul says, "Present yourselves to God as those *who have been brought from death to life,* and your members to God as instruments for righteousness" (Romans 6:13, emphasis added).

"The fruit of the Spirit is love, joy, peace, patience, kindness, goodness, faithfulness, gentleness, self-control; against such things there is no law." And verse 25 says, "If [since] we live by the Spirit, let us also walk by the Spirit [meaning to live our lives by the power of the Holy Spirit]" (Galatians 5:22–23, 25).

John also records for us Jesus's words when he said, "By this my Father is glorified, that you bear much fruit and so prove [confirm] to be my disciples" (John 15:8).

Life itself is a miracle of God, but to be spiritually alive is in some ways like waking up from a dream. It's like the song by Jimmy Cliff that says, "I can see clearly now the rain is gone ... It's gonna be a bright, bright, bright, sunshiny day." It certainly doesn't take away life's difficulties, but it sets them into a whole new realm, a new reality.

❖ RECONCILIATION

For in him all the fullness of God was pleased to dwell,
and through him to reconcile to himself all things,
whether on earth or in heaven, making peace by the blood of his cross.
—Colossians 1:19–20

There is an intriguing suggestion here that Christ's work on the cross will have effects far beyond his salvation of mankind, great as that may be, resulting in removing the effects of sin throughout the entire universe and bringing everlasting peace.

What unfortunately first comes to mind when hearing the word *reconciliation* is marital discord and the high rate of couples being unable or unwilling to reconcile leading inevitably, it seems, to divorce. The dictionary gives the meaning of this word as "to bring into agreement or harmony." It is connected to the word *propitiation*, which we'll look at shortly, in that this bringing together of these two parties, God and man, must also satisfy God's righteous anger against the sin that separates us from him. At times a couple is willing to together go to a counselor, who will act as an intermediator to help them work through their issues and problems in an attempt to mediate a reconciliation. Christ is our unique, one-of-a-kind mediator; Paul wrote, "For there is one God, and there is one mediator between God and men, the man Christ Jesus, who gave himself as a ransom for all" (1 Timothy 2:5–6). We see this idea given more detail in 2 Corinthians 5.

Therefore, if anyone is in Christ, he is a new creation. The old has passed away; behold, the new has come. All this is from God, who through Christ reconciled us to himself and gave us the ministry of reconciliation; that is, *in Christ God was reconciling the world to himself*, not counting their trespasses against them, and entrusting to us the message of reconciliation. Therefore, we are ambassadors for Christ, God making his appeal through us. We implore you on behalf of Christ, be reconciled to God. For our sake he made him to be sin who knew no sin, so that in him we might become the righteousness of God. (2 Corinthians 5:17–21, emphasis added)

This word *reconciliation* (Greek, *apokatallassoo*), used to describe our salvation, suggests the ceasing of hostilities between two parties; in this case, this is between God and us, as human beings. This word and its variations occur fifteen times in the New Testament. "And you, who once were alienated and hostile in mind, doing evil deeds, *he has now reconciled in his body of flesh by his death*, in order to present you holy and blameless and above reproach before him" (Colossians 1:21–22, emphasis added).

It suggests to us that this salvation has made peace between us and God and so enables those reconciled to become part of God's family as well as included and useful in carrying out his eternal plans for humanity. In Romans 5, Paul uses the words "peace with God" in speaking of our reconciliation to God. "Therefore, since we have been justified by faith, *we have peace with God* through our Lord Jesus Christ" (Romans 5:1, emphasis added).

This bringing us back into a relationship with God is at the very heart of the gospel. We often think of our salvation as being about having our sins forgiven and being given eternal life with heaven being our goal. Paul similarly was looking forward to this when he said in 2 Corinthians 5:8–9, "Yes, we are of good courage, and we would rather be away from the body and at home with the Lord."

But God's ultimate goal is to reconcile us back to himself, into a living relationship with him—to restore what was broken in the garden. At present most people's view of God tends to be one characterized by fear and distance. As Christians who have been reconciled to God, we need to seek to enhance this new relationship through reading and studying God's Word and spending time in prayer with him (communicating with God). Paul urges us to do this by "praying at all times in the Spirit, with all prayer and supplication. To that end keep alert with all perseverance, making supplication for all the saints, and also for me" (Ephesians 6:18–19).

But more than that, Paul told the Christians in Corinth that in sharing the message of Christ with others, they were to see themselves as ambassadors, communicating this message, which alone brings reconciliation with God. Second Corinthians 5:17–18, 20, says, "Therefore, if anyone is in Christ, he is a new creation. The old has passed away; behold, the new has come. All this is from God, who through Christ *reconciled us* to himself and gave us *the ministry of reconciliation*; ... Therefore, we are ambassadors for Christ, God making his appeal through us. We implore you on behalf of Christ, *be reconciled to God*" (emphasis added).

In summary, we need to acknowledge just how amazing and complete is this salvation our Lord has provided for us. We've been redeemed by his blood, made free and no longer enslaved to sin and Satan. We have been legally justified (put into a right standing) before God, so our condemnation is gone, and we have been fully forgiven of our sins. Also, we have been spiritually regenerated, made eternally alive to God, so the Holy Spirit can now reside within us. In addition, we have peace with God, being reconciled to him, not only brought near but in fact brought into his very family. Finally, in addition to all this, we see the Father's satisfaction in his Son's work of salvation at Calvary and personally within us in this following section.

◈ PROPITIATION (ROMANS 3:24–25)

> My wrath [will] go forth like fire,
> and burn with none to quench it,
> because of the evil of your deeds.
> —Jeremiah 4:4

I believe one of the greatest errors we can make as human beings is to ignore the fact that our sin incurs the wrath of a holy God.

If you ever went camping in one of our countries wonderful parks, you would have been given literature to read about the safe use of the campsite. One of the main cautions concerns the campfire. In particular, it stresses that you must ensure the fire is completely extinguished before leaving. Even without any visible flame, it can flare up, so one is advised to pour water liberally over the fire.

There's a spiritual application to be made here. Because of his absolute holiness, God's wrath burns toward our sin so that in our natural state we live under his condemnation. The precious blood of Christ alone can fully extinguish or quench it. Going back to the case of the campfire, we see the necessity of water being used to extinguish the fire. But we see different types of extinguishers used for different types of fires: A for common combustibles, B for liquid fires, and C for electrical fires. But for our sins, there is only one that is effective. Paul affirms that we are "justified by his grace as a gift, through the redemption that is in Christ Jesus, whom God put forward as a propitiation *by his blood*" (Romans 3:25, emphasis added).

As the children's chorus says, "What can wash away my sin? / Nothing but the blood of Jesus." That blood is the only extinguisher that will work to quench God's wrath toward us on account of our sin.

This particular word, propitiation, (Greek, *hilaskomi*), seen also in Hebrews 2 and twice in 1 John, isn't one used in our common speech and occurs just these four times in the New Testament. It comes from the Latin *propitiare* and specifically means "to make favorably inclined; to appease; conciliate" (*Thayer's Greek Lexicon* (transliterated). Regarding our salvation, satisfying God's holiness is something man in himself is totally unable to do. "Therefore, [Jesus] had to be made like his brothers in every respect, so that he might become a merciful and faithful high priest in the service of God, *to make propitiation for the sins* of the people" (Hebrews 2:17, emphasis added).

In looking at the terms considered thus far, we see they have focused on the effects of this salvation on us. We have been regenerated, reconciled, and justified. But here the focus is on the effect the sacrificial death of Jesus had on God the Father—how he saw it and continues to see it. First, it was necessary for God to provide an acceptable sacrifice, so it required his Son. Through our Lord's willing sacrifice on behalf of mankind, he was able to fully satisfy God's holiness and his righteous anger regarding our sin and rebellion against him since his sacrifice was of infinite value. Christ Jesus was the only One whose substitutionary death could fully satisfy a holy God. Nothing else would do. No one else could accomplish it. Therefore, God is now able to pardon the sinner and offer to us this gift of forgiveness and salvation (Romans 3:24). And yet, most importantly, he is able to do so without offending his own holiness—expressing his love to us as sinners while remaining holy in himself. Amazing! For those who accept this gift, the condemnation is indeed eternally gone since we're told again in Hebrews, "But when Christ had *offered for all time a single sacrifice for sins,* he sat down at the right hand of God, waiting from that time until his enemies should be made a footstool for his feet. For *by a single offering, he has perfected for all time those who are being sanctified*" (Hebrews 10:12–14, emphasis added).

The old children's hymn by James McGranahan from a century and a half ago gets it right when it says,

> Oh, what a Savior that He died for me!
> From condemnation He hath made me free;
> He that believeth on the Son saith He, Hath everlasting
> life.

The fact that the Lord's sacrifice was of infinite value is why Paul says it is sufficient for all who come. It is of no benefit then to discuss whether he paid a specific price for the specific sins for only "x" number of people. I don't believe we see any indication in Scripture that the punishment our Lord bore at Calvary was based on some mathematical formula or that the punishment he bore was sufficient to cover only the sins of so many people. Instead, what we see is a sacrifice of *limitless value,* something beyond counting. The Father was satisfied with it, and so should we be as well, confident that all who of their free will repent and come to Christ will be saved. Hallelujah to the King of kings, who accomplished such a work!

❖ ADOPTION

> Zion said, "The Lord has forsaken me;
> my Lord has forgotten me."
> "Can a woman forget her nursing child,
> that she should have no compassion on the son of her womb?
> Even these may forget, yet I will not forget you.
> Behold, I have engraved you on the palms of my hands."
> —Isaiah 49:14–16

The word *adoption* is used for the act of making someone legally your child. Today, it presupposes that the child doesn't have parents or at least parents who are able or willing to care for him or her and that the adoptive couple want this child. For the child in this initial situation, it often causes deep feelings of abandonment and of being unloved. Adoption then can be a wonderful thing, bringing with it a longed-for sense of love and security. Looking in the Scriptures, we see how this word is applied in a spiritual sense, since God has done this for us.

> I mean that the heir, as long as he is a child, is no different from a slave, though he is the owner of everything, but he is under guardians and managers until the date set by his father. In the same way we also, when we were children, were enslaved to the elementary principles of the world. But when the fullness of time had come, God sent forth his Son, born of woman, born under the law, to redeem those who were under the law, so that we might *receive adoption as sons. And because you are sons, God has sent the Spirit of his Son into our hearts, crying, "Abba! Father!"* So, you are no longer a slave, but a son, and if a son, then an heir through God. (Galatians 4:1–7, emphasis added)

In Genesis 17 we see God entering into a covenant relationship with Abraham and all his descendants, legally binding himself to them as a nation to be their God and heavenly Father and to give them an inheritance, the land of Canaan, for an everlasting possession. Essentially, God was adopting them nationally as his children. And he will keep his word in this regard. He will not forget his promises. See God's words to Abraham. "And I will establish my covenant between me and you and your offspring after you throughout their generations for *an everlasting covenant*, to be God to you and to your offspring after you. And I will give to you and to your offspring after you the land of your sojournings, all the land of Canaan, for *an everlasting possession*, and I will be their God" (Genesis 17:7–8).

Paul picks up on this in Romans when listing all the blessings Israel had come into through this unique relationship. He says, "They are Israelites, and to them belong *the adoption*, the glory, the covenants, the giving of the law, the worship, and the promises" (Romans 9:4, emphasis added).

This national adoption, however, didn't extend individually to Jews who didn't follow God or obey his law. The beggar and the rich man, from the story the Lord told in Luke 16, were both Jews, but in death, Lazarus was carried by the angels to Abraham's bosom, and the rich man was buried, no doubt with great pomp and fanfare, but found himself in Hades. Paul, in talking about individual Jewish people, clarifies this theology by writing, "For no one is a Jew who is merely one outwardly, nor is circumcision outward and physical. But a Jew is one inwardly, and circumcision is a matter of the heart, by the Spirit, not by the letter. His praise [then], is not from man but from God" (Romans 2:28–29).

Coming to the New Testament, we read about the wonderful news of the gospel, salvation offered to all through the shed blood of Jesus. God extended an invitation to all people to individually put their faith in this finished work, as we read in Romans 3:23–25. Then Paul lists for us in chapter 5 the many blessings that are ours due to being justified by God—peace with God, a new standing of grace before him, and the indwelling of the Holy Spirit, to name a few. He then follows up on this redemption by telling us what has happened to those who have been saved and indwelt with his Spirit.

Here are two passages that talk about this adoption. We read that new Gentile believers in the churches of Galatia were being persuaded by proselytizing Jews to keep the Old Testament laws. Paul calls this teaching heretical, useless, and no longer relevant since Christ has come. See what he tells them about this. "So then, the law was our guardian until Christ came, in order that we might be justified by faith. But now that faith has come, we are no longer under a guardian, for in Christ Jesus you are all *sons of God*, through faith" (Galatians 3:24–26, emphasis added).

Then we see Paul in Romans 8 telling us again what it means for a Christian to be a son of God. "For all who are led by the Spirit of God are *sons of God*. For you did not receive the spirit of slavery to fall back into fear, but *you have received the Spirit of adoption as sons, by whom we cry, 'Abba! Father!'* The Spirit himself bears witness with our spirit that *we are children of God*, and if children, then heirs—heirs of God and fellow heirs with Christ" (Romans 8:14–17, emphasis added).

The use of this interesting word *Abba* from the Aramaic language infers a relationship of real closeness and trust of the father within a family. More than only being freed from the slavery of sin, great as that may be, and more even than just being able to call God our Father in some official capacity, we have become members of his family and heirs of his promises. We have a heavenly Father and are part of his eternal family. How wonderful that we have this very real identity as his sons and daughters, and what security this gives and what a future! Paul tells us that "we will also reign with him" (2 Timothy 2:12), thus indicating the extent of this sonship.

Scripture tells us that, having been cleansed from our sins and justified by the blood of Jesus, we have been reconciled to God. That being true, the Father has now adopted us into the family of God with the seal of it being the indwelling of God's Holy Spirit within us. Enjoy the truth of these lyrics written by Gloria Gaither.

> I then shall live as one who's been forgiven.
> I'll walk with joy to know my debts are paid.
> I know my name is clear before my Father;
> I am His child, and I am not afraid.
> So, greatly pardoned, I'll forgive my brother;
> The law of love I gladly will obey.

Chapter Two

The Means and Application of this Salvation

◆ GRACE

> Marvelous grace of our loving Lord,
> Grace that exceeds our sin and our guilt!
> Yonder on Calvary's mount outpoured
> There where the blood of Lamb was spilt.
> —Julia H. Johnston

Let's now leave the study of the word *salvation* and all its corollaries and move on to how we can experience it for ourselves with a study of another list of biblical terms. Not unexpectedly it starts with God taking the initiative. Romans 6:23 says, "For the wages of sin is death, but *the free gift of God* is eternal life in Christ Jesus our Lord" (emphasis added). It may seem odd to start with a verse that doesn't seem to contain the word being discussed. However, it does contain the noun from which it comes and the essence of its meaning—an undeserved gift, freely given (Greek, *charis*), an act of generous goodness toward another.

The word *grace* is used in the New Testament in several different senses, but God's grace always speaks to us of his freely given divine favor toward us. Grace in Scripture finds its origin in God's love, which he is in his very essence; John says in 1 John 4:8, "God is love." Having become fallen through Adam and now having a sin nature within, we are separated from God because of that sin and are wholly unworthy in ourselves to be in his presence, yet amazingly he still loves us. See what Paul writes in his letter to the Ephesians: "But God, being rich in mercy, because of the great love with which he loved us, even when we were dead in our trespasses, made us alive together with Christ—*by grace you have been saved*" (Ephesians 2:4–5, emphasis added).

So we see God acting in favor toward us not because we have earned it but because of his love toward us. Even our "good deeds" are tainted by our motives. Psalm 53 sums up this idea from the viewpoint of a holy God looking down on us. "God looks down from heaven on the children of man to see if there are any who understand, who seek after God. They have all fallen away; together they have become corrupt; there is none who does good, not even one" (Psalm 53:2–3).

Lest we think this assessment is overly severe, we must remember that God's comparison here isn't of one person against another but of someone being compared to the holiness and purity of God. James writes, "For whoever keeps the whole law but fails in one point has become accountable for all of it" (James 2:10). The real question then is this: Why should God love us at all and in his love show us his favor, his abundant grace, in providing this extravagant gift of salvation?

Let's look back at Genesis, where we see the power of creation as God spoke the world and all its parts into existence on each successive day. Each of these acts started with the words "And God said." But then on the sixth day, after God created the animals, we see "Then God said let us make man in our image, after our likeness" (Genesis 1:26), indicating a difference from what had gone before in all his creative acts, wonderful as they were.

Here was a creative act that was not only different but also different in kind from all that had gone before—making, out of flesh and blood, self-aware living beings capable of love, like himself, and with an eternal spirit, tripartite beings, reflecting God's own image! He made us because in his love he had future plans for us, desiring that we should be able to freely choose to be in an eternal, loving relationship with him, the eternal I AM, the almighty One, the triune God.

There is a similarity here to the story concerning Adam that we read in Genesis 2. It says that God gave him the task of naming the animals. We read, "The man gave names to all livestock and to the birds of the heavens and to every beast of the field." But then the sentence ends with these interesting words: "But for Adam there was not found *a helper fit for him*" (Genesis 2:20, emphasis added).

And so it was with God himself; after all the majesty of his creation, even up to and making the animals, we could interject this quote about Adam from chapter 2 and apply it to God. "There was not found a helper [within this creation] fit for him." It required a special act of creation to make mankind, both man and woman, in his own image. We must not suppose, of course, that God lacked anything, complete as he was in the perfect triunity of his own persons: Father, Son, and Holy Spirit. But in his love, he chose to create new beings, human beings, to whom he could extend that love. What is suggested here in this second chapter of Genesis is seen in its full amazing reality in the second last chapter of Revelation. "And I saw the holy city, new Jerusalem, coming down out of heaven from God, prepared as *a bride adorned for her husband*. And I heard a loud voice from the throne saying, 'Behold, the dwelling place of God is with man'" (Revelation 21:2–3, emphasis added).

After the fall, however, we see our complete inability to do works worthy of righteousness that we might, by our own efforts, restore that broken relationship and truly be "a helper fit for him," to love and be loved. Instead, we see God reaching out to us, his created though fallen creatures. As John says in his much-loved words, "For God so loved the world, that he gave his only Son, that whoever believes in him should not perish but have eternal life" (John 3:16). We see the Son of God actually taking on our humanity and then giving up that human life so we, human beings made in his image, might have eternal life and be brought once again into a relationship with him. That's God's amazing grace, though undeserved, and a true expression of his deep love for us.

Some have called this grace an unfathomable mystery and something hidden within the secrets of God's own counsels to be bestowed on a select few. But we must realize that grace is an expression of God's love—one of the principal attributes of his character. God in his essential being is a trinity, which is a mystery to us. But in this eternal fellowship between the Father, Son, and Holy Spirit, as revealed in Scripture, we see that love, that essential core attribute of his being, perfectly expressed between the persons of the Trinity. And in his choosing to make man in his own image, he was intentionally setting about to expand the circle of that love. He created us so we might experience it, reflect it, and through it join in a relationship with him. And having planned to do this, he would not let man's marring it derail his plan by sin, causing it to fail, no matter the cost involved. Peter revealed his desire to us and told us just how patient God is with us, "not wishing that any should perish, but that all should reach repentance" (2 Peter 3:9); and if repentance, then salvation. And if salvation, then renewed fellowship with him.

Yet while creating us to be able to love and enjoy fellowship with him, at the same time he made us moral creatures with free will and the capacity to choose our way in this world with the ability to decide either to accept the gift provided or to turn away from him. That's why God in Genesis 2 presented to Adam the two trees and then spoke of his obedience as a moral choice. Genesis 3 clearly tells us about Adam and Eve's moral awareness. Immediately after disobeying God's command, they felt the acute guilt of this disobedience and made a fumbling attempt to fix it. And God found them culpable of their action of sinning against him as he continues to do with our wrong choices even today.

Paul tells us of our state before salvation. "You were dead in the trespasses and sins in which you once walked [cut off from a relationship with God]" (Ephesians 2:1–2). And now in that state of separation from God, of being "spiritually dead," we are also cut off from God's wisdom in our hearts because of our sin. Clearly this deadness refers to our total inability to reconcile ourselves to God and in no way denies the awareness of sin or the ability to accept by faith God's offer of salvation for us. See this fundamental salvation passage again as Paul wrote it. "For all have sinned and fall short of the glory of God, and are justified by his grace as a gift, through the redemption that is in Christ Jesus, whom God put forward as a propitiation by his blood, *to be received by faith*" (Romans 3:23–25, emphasis added).

In addition to this darkness within us, Satan desperately tries to prevent us from responding to this offer of grace by blinding us to God's truth. In 2 Corinthians we read this rather shocking truth. "The god of this world [Satan] has blinded the minds of the unbelievers, to keep them from seeing the light of the gospel of the glory of Christ, who is the image of God" (2 Corinthians 4:4). That would seem to imply our certain doom, but then just two verses later, we read in verse 6, "For God, who said, 'Let light shine out of darkness,' [speaking here of creation] has shone in our hearts [through the Spirit] to give the light of the knowledge of the glory of God in the face of Jesus Christ" (2 Corinthians 4:6).

This makes me want to shout, "Checkmate!" This is the Spirit's work in the world and in our hearts, which more than counteracts Satan's plans. Despite the devil's best efforts, John tells us in the opening verses of his Gospel that the power of God's light through his Spirit is stronger than Satan's darkness. "In him [Jesus, the Son of God] was life, and the life was the light of men. The light shines in the darkness, and the darkness has not overcome it [i.e., can never vanquish or extinguish it]" (John 1:4–5).

Speaking further of the Holy Spirit and how he works in people's hearts, we see the Lord telling his disciples in John 16 that in leaving them as he returned to heaven, he would send the Holy Spirit into the world to convict people of their sin. Earlier in John 6, we are told that God the Father will use the Holy Spirit to pull on our hearts and consciences, drawing us toward him. The Scripture says, "No one can come to me unless the Father who sent me draws [pulls on] him" (John 6:44). There is no indication here of the Spirit of God dragging us against our will or alternatively of there being something selective in this universal task as John 16 says. "And when he [the Holy Spirit] comes, he will convict the world concerning sin and righteousness and judgment" (John 16:8–9).

Despite our sinful natures, we aren't brute beasts, but we have been given within us a spirit and thus a God-consciousness, moral nature, and free will; as we saw on the previous page from Romans 3:23, we can personally make choices as we live in this world. And these attributes haven't been lost despite the fall of man. Story after story in the Old

Testament shows situations where God presents a moral choice, and we get to see man's response. The first of these was Adam and Eve in the Garden of Eden where they chose to disobey. Another story is found in Genesis 6 about Noah. In a culture where "the wickedness of man was great in the earth, and that every intention of the thoughts of his heart was only evil continually" (Genesis 6:5), we're told that Noah chose to follow God. The Scripture says of him in verse 9, "Noah was a righteous man, blameless in his generation. Noah walked with God." The stories of these moral decisions go on throughout the Scriptures. In Hebrews 11 we see a list of those who chose to follow God despite the difficulties this brought. In Psalms 32 and 51, David lays bare his choice of sinning and feelings of guilt before a holy God before finding the joy of forgiveness through repentance. But what a cost it was to him, even one so dear to God's heart.

The Spirit can still work in our hearts, sinful as they are, to convict us; and we can in turn still respond to him and place our faith in Jesus. He can use many means to draw us to himself, but he does so most particularly through the written and living Word of God, the two-edged sword described in Hebrew 4:12. And as people respond to the Spirit's work in their hearts, they are able, as beings made in God's image, to respond in faith and lives are transformed by the grace of God and the power of the Spirit working in them.

Salvation involves the entirety of the Trinity of God. Paul emphasizes this in the introductory verses of his gospel opus to the Roman believers.

> Paul, a servant of Christ Jesus, called to be an apostle, set apart for the *gospel of God*, which he promised beforehand through his prophets in the holy Scriptures, *concerning his Son*, who was descended from David according to the flesh and was declared to be the Son of God in power according to *the Spirit of holiness* by his resurrection from the dead, Jesus Christ our Lord. (Romans 1:1–4, emphasis added)

The Father planned it. The Son needed to become incarnate, taking on our humanity and so die for us. The Holy Spirit was involved in the Lord's resurrection and his present work to counteract Satan's deception by convicting us in our consciences of our sin and our need and God's love for us. In addition, upon our believing, the Father restores us to spiritual life and places us in his family. Then in addition to this life-giving work, the Holy Spirit indwells us and continues his ongoing work of sanctification within us throughout the remainder of our lives. And finally, we are given the assurance that if we falter or fail in this life. The Son himself is our Advocate before the Father for us. John says, "My little children, I am writing these things to you so that you may not sin. But if anyone does sin, we have an advocate with the Father, Jesus Christ the righteous" (1 John 2:1–2). What an amazing *work of grace* it is!

The opposite of receiving this gift of salvation offered by God's grace is rejecting it or trying to earn it ourselves. Our natural human response to the guilt caused by our separation from God has produced so much religious effort over millennia past to do our own "works of righteousness" (Titus 3:5). These are vain attempts to make ourselves acceptable to God, to bridge the gap caused by our sin. This phrase represents the long, fruitless efforts of people to accomplish their own salvation. And the Scriptures clearly show us it is an impossible task. But the work of Christ was different, satisfying the utter holiness of his Father, as we read in Hebrews 10. "And every priest stands daily at his service, offering repeatedly the same sacrifices [human effort], *which can never take away sins.* But when Christ had offered for all time a single sacrifice for sins, he sat down at the right hand of God, waiting from that time until his enemies should be made a footstool for his feet" (vv. 11–13, emphasis added).

In addition, as mentioned above, Paul clearly states, "For *by grace* you have been saved through faith. And this is not your own doing; it is the gift of God, *not a result of works*, so that no one may boast" (Ephesians 2:8–9, emphasis added). The work is all indeed of God, but the choice is ours. The offer is before each one. What a serious thought! Let me conclude this section with the last verse of William Newell's hymn "At Calvary" (note my emphasis on the second line), which we'll look at again in the next section,

O the love that drew salvation's plan!
O *the grace* that brought it down to man!
O the mighty gulf that God did span at Calvary.

The question then is this. How can I say thanks and express my gratitude to God for showing me such undeserved favor? Surely it should first be in the way I live my life by reflecting that grace in the way I treat others. It will be a selfless, countercultural way of life, and people, though not necessarily understanding it, will be drawn to it.

◆ FAITH

My faith has found a resting place, not in device or creed
I trust the Ever-living One, His wounds for me shall plead.
I need no other argument; I need no other plea;
It is enough that Jesus died, and that He died for me.
—Lidie H. Edmunds

Scripture tells us that salvation can be personally ours through an act of faith or believing or putting our trust in God. It's an act of our personal will, of simply reaching out in our need to receive this gift God offers, as we see in Romans 3.

> But now the righteousness of God has been manifested apart from the law, although the Law and the Prophets bear witness to it— the righteousness of God *through faith in Jesus Christ for all who believe.* For there is no distinction: for all have sinned and fall short of the glory of God, and are justified by his grace as a gift, through the redemption that is in Christ Jesus, whom God put forward as a propitiation by his blood, *to be received by faith.* This was to show God's righteousness, because in his divine forbearance he had passed over former sins. It was to show his righteousness at the present time, so that he might be just and the justifier of *the one who has faith in Jesus.* (Romans 3:21–26, emphasis added)

I've already quoted from this passage (obviously a favorite!), but this time I do so to show God's expectation as to our response. The word *faith* (Greek, *pistos*), mentioned three times here, means to be firmly persuaded or to put one's trust in or receive that which one believes to be true. We'll start the study of this word by looking at the example of the woman who touched the hem of the Lord's garment, as recounted in all three Synoptic Gospels. "For she said to herself, 'If I only touch his garment, I will be made well.' Jesus turned, and seeing her he said, 'Take heart, daughter; your faith has made you well.' And instantly the woman was made well" (Matthew 9:21–23).

Jesus said it was her faith that had made her well, but the question then is this. What was it about that faith that could have cured her? Was there any miraculous saving power in her faith, or was it because of the greatness of her faith, or was it instead the object of her faith that made it effectual? Actually, she did have faith; she believed or was firmly convinced that Jesus could make her well, but it was in whom her faith was placed that made all the difference. It was Jesus, the Son of God, who miraculously healed her.

Faith is a simple word meaning to have trust or confidence in something or someone. But it's an important word, occurring 250 times alone in the New Testament, and it is central to our discussion on salvation. Nowhere in all these instances is there a suggestion that faith is blind or irrational or something to be acted on *despite the facts* or, lastly, even something we no longer have that must be supplied by God.

Take the example of Jesus's invitation to Peter to come to him by walking on the water. By faith, Peter jumped from the boat and started walking on the water to Jesus. But when he looked around at the storm, he panicked and began sinking. We know the story of how Jesus saved him. But then he asked Peter, "O you of little faith, *why did you doubt?*" (Matthew 14:31, emphasis added). I suppose most people reading these words would think that doubting would actually seem like the most reasonable response in the world. People just don't walk on water!

So why did Jesus say this? For context, we need to go back earlier in chapter 14 where we see that Jesus, with just five loaves of bread and two fish, fed over five thousand people until they were completely full. What a great miracle! Later that same day in the evening, Jesus asked

Peter to join him out on the water in the middle of a storm, but he had only a few hours before showed Peter the power of his deity and what he could do with the little food provided So within the context of that day, it was eminently reasonable that he would ask Peter why he doubted. And Peter's initial faith, based on seeing the feeding of five thousand people, was also eminently reasonable. Interestingly, we also see the power of deity, which was allowed to be constrained by Peter's lack of faith.

Over two years before this, Jesus had called Peter and Andrew and then James and John to be his disciples as they were fishing on the Sea of Galilee. He said to them, "Follow me." This wasn't the first time they had seen or heard him, but now it was decision time. Believing something was likely to be true wasn't sufficient; it required action, a step of faith.

The writer of Hebrews devotes one whole chapter (11) to define and then illustrate from the Old Testament this wonderful concept called "faith" and the actions that inevitably followed from it. Verses 1 and 5 give us the essential definition. "Now faith is the *assurance* of things hoped for, the *conviction* of things not seen" (emphasis added). And then in verse 5, we find, "And without faith it is impossible to please him, for whoever would draw near to God must *believe that he exists and that he rewards those who seek him*" (emphasis added).

This was a belief not only in the existence of God but also in his immanence, a God actively engaged within this world for our benefit.

The remainder of this chapter in Hebrews then goes on to illustrate that this confidence by these heroes of the faith was indeed a reasonable confidence in the Creator God and in his plans for their good. What is truly remarkable is that during their lifetimes, these people of faith often didn't, for the most part, see the fulfillment of the things for which they confidently waited. Yet their conviction rested on their understanding of God's character of love and goodness, as revealed through his previous acts and the earlier fulfillment of his promises. They understood he was a covenant-keeping God and that he was good.

The criteria of that faith were first (v. 5) to believe that God *exists*, and there was plenty of evidence all around for that; and second, to believe that he rewards *those who seek him*. The history of the people of Israel was brimming with stories of God being good and helping his people out of their difficulties and trouble. It wasn't that these people never doubted. David wrote in his very personal Psalm 73 about doubting when he saw the prosperity of so many wicked people. But then God opened his eyes to see their end, and his faith was restored.

The hope or confidence of these people described in Hebrews 11, however, was pre-eminently in the promised coming Messiah, in Jesus, *Yeshua* (transliteration of the Hebrew phrase "Jehovah saves"). The author concludes his discussion of faith in the first two verses of the next chapter, starting with his "therefore" that we should be (as they were) looking to him and for him. "Therefore, since we are surrounded by so great a cloud of witnesses, let us also lay aside every weight, and sin which clings so closely, and let us run with endurance the race that is set before us, looking to Jesus, the founder and perfecter [fulfiller] of our faith, who for the joy that was set before him endured the cross, despising the shame, and is seated at the right hand of the throne of God" (Hebrews 12:1–2).

The inference here is that by sitting down at the right hand of the Father, his work of redemption was complete, and he was now, on the basis of this finished work, able to completely fulfill the promises given to these people of faith. God was the One who had planned this great salvation, and then our Lord Jesus brought it about in a most remarkable way by coming into our world (called the "incarnation"). And as a human being, he died for us all—thus becoming the justifier of their faith and of ours today. Now on his throne, at the right hand of the Father, he will be the security for it.

Their confidence or trust in God and his promises, a synonym for faith, and their resultant actions were the necessary ingredients for their names being recorded in this chapter. But it was not an irrational faith, for they could look at the world around them and at God's work in it up to the time of their own lives, revealing his attributes to them; they took confidence through his past works among them and his sure promises to them.

The first example given in this faith chapter is that of a young man of faith named Abel, the second son of Adam and Eve, whose sacrifice was more acceptable than that of his brother Cain. Why was that? Could it be that he knew that what was expected was based on his knowledge of God's previous actions in the garden? He would have heard about the sacrifice God made for his parents when the Lord provided coverings for their nakedness through the skins of slain animals. So he knew what God required as an atonement for sin and that he needed to do this as well. This was not just some coming-of-age ceremony, but now at an age of accountability, he was to come before God because of his own sin. In an age when people didn't need to kill animals for food, it wouldn't have been easy to take the life of a lamb, but in obedience he did so. He trusted that God was real and that this was God's way to atone for his transgressions. Read for yourself the other stories of faith in Hebrew 11, fifteen named and many others referenced.

So it was certainly not an irrational faith, but neither was it an easy faith, because Satan, being the god of this world, made it extremely difficult for them. Not only did they need to work hard to survive on this cursed earth, but they were also tempted by the devil to sin and show contempt for God and man alike. Nevertheless, those who believed in God—first Abel and then these people of faith who followed— persevered and were by God's grace included for all time in his list of faith heroes.

Personal faith or belief in God and his redemptive work remains for us today a necessary component of our salvation, and it is something we must freely choose to do. It begs the question as to why these people, mentioned in this particular chapter, should be listed as examples for us to follow if, as one theological system maintains, God had chosen them to do this and implanted this belief in their hearts through no decision or choice of their own.

The last verses I'd like us to consider here regarding faith are found in Ephesians. "For by grace you *have been saved* through faith. And this is not your own doing; it [this salvation] is the gift of God, not a result of works, so that no one may boast" (Ephesians 2:8, emphasis added). Grace reaches out to give the gift freely provided, and in response, faith reaches out to take it. Careful exegesis would tell us that it is being "saved" that is the gift and the focus of Paul's thoughts in this passage and that it's this salvation that isn't the result of works. This is similar to verse 5 where Paul states that being made "alive together with Christ" was likewise not a result of works but of God's grace. "But God ... even when we were dead in our trespasses, made us alive together with Christ—by grace you *have been saved*" (Ephesians 2:4–5, emphasis added).

Harold Hoehner, past Distinguished professor of New Testament studies at Dallas Theological Seminary, in his exegetical commentary on Ephesians explains the above phrase by saying, "And *toutos "this"* is not your own doing…" in it this way…

> Some commentators think that it may refer to "faith," the nearest preceding noun. A serious objection to this is that the feminine noun does not match the neuter gender of the pronoun. The same problem is raised with "grace," a feminine noun…. Rather than any particular word it is best to conclude that *toutos* refers back to the preceding section. This is common and there are numerous illustrations of such in Ephesians. For example, in 1:15 "this" refers back to the contents 1:3-14, in 3:1 it refers back to 2:11-22 and in 3:14 it refers back to 3:1-13. Therefore in the present context *toutos* refers back to 2:4-8a and more specifically 2:8a, the concept of salvation by grace through faith.[7]

Therefore, although salvation can never be earned by our works, it's likewise true that faith in itself isn't a work. Both God's active and amazing grace on our behalf and our simple faith in opening our hearts to receive it are therefore necessary.

Here it would be good to consider the problem of "doubt." Although creatures of eternity, we are also creatures of time and space with all the limitations of frail humanity. God isn't surprised that we have doubts or even at times may doubt him. Doubt is an insidious thing, draining away our energy and will. All the disciples had times of doubt, as did many of the great men of faith down through the ages. Remember the classic story in Mark of a father pleading with Jesus to cure his son, who suffered from demon possession. "'But if you can do anything, have compassion on us and help us.' And Jesus said to him, 'If you can! All things are possible for one who believes.' Immediately the father of the child cried out and said, 'I believe; help my unbelief!'" (Mark 9:22–24).

What a revealing and honest reply! Although the disciples hadn't been able to help and the man wasn't completely sure of the outcome, after receiving the rebuke from Jesus about his "if you can!" statement, he committed himself to accept Jesus's help. The outcome of course was that Jesus banished the evil spirit, and the boy was made well.

Also, we must remember that we live in a world in rebellion toward God, with Satan himself sowing the seeds of doubt in our minds, as he did with Eve in the garden. But God doesn't expect us, in believing in him, to just take a blind leap of faith. We can clearly see his omnipotence in Creation. And in the Scriptures, we repeatedly see that our God is a faithful, promise-keeping God. Beyond all that, because of his love, his Son died for us for our eternal salvation. It's also evident that God has given to us rational minds able to think logically about these eternal verities.

Billy Graham tells of the time, near the beginning of his preaching ministry, when one of his best friends, a gifted evangelist, turned away from the faith; this caused him to seriously question himself and his own faith. He read the Scriptures, prayed, and looked back over his life up to that point and came to the "logical decision," he wrote later[8], to place his faith once again and for the remainder of his life in the Savior, who loved him and had died for him. Perhaps that's why he emphasized the word *decision* so much during his preaching. He even called his radio messages *The Hour of Decision*.

As rational people, we can think things through and evaluate the truth of what we hear and understand. But at some point, we need to choose what we accept and what we believe to be true and move forward based on that conviction. Below we see the Lord's parting command to his disciples as he was leaving them. While there was some initial doubt, all his disciples ended up being willing to die for him and spend their lives carrying out his Great Commission. Read what Matthew tells us.

> Now the eleven disciples went to Galilee, to the mountain to which Jesus had directed them. And when they saw him, they worshiped him, *but some doubted.* And Jesus came and said to them, "All authority in heaven and on earth has been given to me. Go therefore and make disciples of all nations, baptizing them in the name of the Father and of the Son and of the Holy Spirit,

teaching them to observe all that I have commanded you. And behold, I am with you always, to the end of the age." (Matthew 28:16–20, emphasis added)

And on the strength of his promise to them, they threw themselves into the work of making disciples until, with all but John, their work came to an end by their martyrdom.

◆ CONVICTION AND REPENTANCE

Years I spent in vanity and pride,
Caring not my Lord was crucified,
Knowing not it was for me He died on Calvary.

By God's Word at last my sin I learned,
Then I trembled at the law I'd spurned,
Till my guilty soul imploring turned to Calvary

Mercy there was great, and grace was free,
Pardon there was multiplied to me,
There my burdened soul found liberty
At Calvary.

—William R. Newell

See now again this old hymn favourite, but particularly the words of the second verse of Newell's hymn. He wrote that it was Scripture, "God's Word" that broke through his careless indifference. Conviction of sin is the work of God's Spirit in the heart of a morally conscious human being. In our modern world, this word is generally used in the context of a judge or jury handing down a verdict and the accused being found guilty. If we follow this order, there will be a sentence served appropriate to the crime.

Instead, spiritual conviction comes to each individual first from within, since the Holy Spirit uses the moral compass within each of us and also from the Word of God. Paul calls the Scripture the "sword of the Spirit," for it is God's Spirit that powerfully uses the living Word in our hearts. So God's Spirit urges us to accept the truth about ourselves and our guilt and to act on it.

Paul says of people who didn't know or follow the Law as given to Moses that they still possessed that common moral code. "They show that the work of the law is written on their hearts, while their conscience also bears witness" (Romans 2:15). It tells us that groups of people throughout the world, no matter the distance or isolation from one another, have within them a similar moral code much like the Ten Commandments of the Old Testament or the Golden Rule of the New Testament. The reason for this is clear, since God made us as morally conscious beings, having an innate understanding of right and wrong, which he, our Maker, placed there. Evolutionists struggle to make sense of this since they believe we are only physical material beings like all the rest of life, living life in survival mode of survival of the fittest. However, our consciences are a trigger God gave in our spirits to warn us when we swerve from his ways. The knowledge of God's love or kindness, as Romans 2:4 says, "is meant to lead you to repentance," leading us back to him. This love, in addition to the consciousness of sin, is together meant to turn us around, drawing us back to him in repentance.

Unfortunately, when people choose to repeatedly ignore and knowingly resist their consciences and the gracious work of the Spirit in their hearts, then, as Titus 1:15 says, "their consciences are defiled," and they become increasingly insensitive to what is right or wrong. This downward spiral will progress if conscience continues to be ignored, as Paul writes to Timothy (1 Timothy 4), and the result will be a "seared" (or unfeeling) conscience. Eventually, Peter says in 2 Peter 2:12 that they become "like irrational animals, creatures of instinct, born to be caught and destroyed." What an indictment of people created in the image of God, who have the purpose of living in loving and holy fellowship with him! Paul concludes Romans 1 with the same accusation, the inevitable ending of this downward spiral.

> And since they did not see fit to acknowledge God, God gave them up to a debased mind to do what ought not to be done. They were filled with all manner of

> unrighteousness, evil, covetousness, malice. They are full of envy, murder, strife, deceit, maliciousness. They are gossips, slanderers, haters of God, insolent, haughty, boastful, inventors of evil, disobedient to parents, foolish, faithless, heartless, ruthless. Though they know God's decree that those who practice such things deserve to die, they not only do them but give approval to those who practice them. (Romans 1:28–32)

Let us quickly turn away from that horrific picture and look instead at the related word *repentance*. This word speaks to an expected response that ought to come from a person because of that conviction, as seen above. It ought to be a natural response in each of us as moral beings, when having our eyes opened spiritually, to see ourselves in all our sinfulness as compared to God's holiness. Paul sums up for us the natural course of a person's life while living in the world without God when he tells the Ephesian believers, "And you were dead in the trespasses and sins in which you once walked, following the course of this world, following the prince of the power of the air" (Ephesians 2:1–2).

To repent (Greek, *metanoeo*) means to turn away from following the way leading to perdition, a lost eternity, and to turn in a new direction and toward someone else, namely to God. In his first great sermon on the day of Pentecost, Peter said, "*Repent* therefore, and *turn again*, that your sins may be blotted out" (Acts 3:19, emphasis added). It requires me to make a choice about my life and the way it is going—turning away from Satan's ways and my way and turning to Christ and accepting his way and his salvation. The Lord tells us there is no salvation without repentance. "Unless you repent, you will all likewise perish" (Luke 13:5). So there must be a change of heart about us and God.

Repentance isn't a superficial thing, something done on a whim, but it means a personal assessment has occurred, and we have found ourselves lacking, coming to the grim conclusion that we are spiritually lost and, in fact, hopelessly so. It means acknowledging the truth of what the Holy Spirit has been revealing and convicting us about ourselves. Whether this involves great spiritual turmoil and struggle or for a young child simply to accept the truth of God's Word about him or herself; it is a necessary first step in receiving Christ as our Savior.

It's important to understand that "to repent" implies more than simply "to regret" or have a change of mind because of the negative effect on themselves when people get caught or found out. One good example of regret seen in Scripture is in 1 Samuel 15, when Samuel accosted Saul about his disobedience to God's command regarding the battle with the Amalekites. When reminded of God's clear commands, Saul acknowledged to Samuel that he had sinned but then immediately requested that Samuel act before the people as if everything were fine between them. His first thought was still about himself and about looking good before others.

Another example is Judas Iscariot in the New Testament. After seeing Jesus arrested, he was taken by surprise that this time the Lord had allowed himself to be taken into custody. I would suggest that his plan may have been just to make a little money on the side and then step back as Jesus brought to nothing all the evil plans of man, as had previously happened. There had been a pattern of unscrupulous behavior as Scripture affirms when saying that "he was a thief and having charge of the moneybag he used to help himself to what was put into it" (John 12:6). However, this time things were different. "Then when Judas, his betrayer, saw that Jesus was condemned, he *changed his mind* and brought back the thirty pieces of silver to the chief priests and the elders, saying, 'I have sinned by betraying innocent blood.' They said, 'What is that to us? See to it yourself'" (Matthew 27:3–5).

We shouldn't interpret this as meaning that he was here turning to God in genuine contrition, but instead, like Saul, we see him still trying to make the best of a bad situation; only this time he saw no way out. He regretted or changed his mind about what he had done because of how this was going to affect him personally. That is regret; unlike repentance, it didn't lead to salvation because he didn't turn to God. We see the solemn conclusion of the story; when referencing his death by suicide, Luke says, "Judas turned aside to go to his own place" (Acts 1:9). It was his own place because that was what he had truly chosen.

We see then that it is only true conviction focused on our broken relationship with God that can lead to true repentance, a change of heart. Then by confessing sin and throwing ourselves, as it were, on his mercy, we will find salvation. That's why John says in his first epistle, "If we confess our sins, he is faithful and just to forgive us our sins and to cleanse us from all unrighteousness" (1 John 1:9).

It seems that Judas didn't know God or understand his character of love and doubtless never thought that he'd receive mercy if he even did dare to ask. Remember the contrast of the words of the tax collector in Luke 18:13. "God, be merciful to me, a sinner!" Here Judas didn't turn back to God in repentance. We read, "Throwing down the pieces of silver into the temple, he departed, and he went and hanged himself" (Matthew 27:5).

Remember, when turning to the Lord in true repentance, we will always experience God's loving heart expressed in receiving us back to himself. Never forget that.

◆ FORGIVENESS

> God forgave my sin in Jesus' name,
> I've been born again in Jesus' name;
> And in Jesus' name I come to you
> To share His love as He told me to.
> —Carol Owens

Though this was mentioned earlier, it would be good to think further about forgiveness and particularly God's forgiveness of our sins. Let me quote again from John Bunyan, the early English evangelist, who was in jail in Bedford, England, because of his unauthorized outdoor preaching in 1678. There in the "gaol" (as the jail was then called) he wrote his famous allegory *The Pilgrim's Progress*. The story is about a man called Christian, who was making his way toward the celestial city and carrying on his back a great burden. Many of his friends made fun of his decision to start on this journey, but he persisted despite many obstacles along the way. This great burden he carried, Bunyan tells us, represented the great load of guilt he felt on account of his sins. Listen to what Bunyan wrote (in modernized English).

> Now I saw in my dream that the road, from then on, was fenced in on either side with a wall. The wall was named Salvation. Along the road did burdened Christian run. Or should we say, he did his best to run, so far as he could, with that load upon his back. He ran till he came to a small hill, at the top of which stood a cross and at the bottom of which was a tomb. I saw in my dream that when Christian walked up the hill to the wayside cross its shadow fell across him. Suddenly the burden, slipping from his shoulders, fell from off his back, tumbling down the hill until it came to the mouth of the tomb, where it fell in to be seen no more.[2]

This section of Bunyan's book finishes, as mentioned in part earlier, by saying, "Great dangers lay ahead of him but for the moment he was as light as air. So, Christian gave three leaps for joy and went on singing."

What a great picture of the joy of any person who has just come to realize his or her sins were all forgiven by a holy God! The very essence of this joy lies in those who know their guilt, seek forgiveness, and come to the realization that the debt causing the separation between them and God has been fully paid.

When looking at the use of this word in the New Testament, we see two main Greek words that are close in meaning but with distinct emphasis and connotation. The first word, *aphesis* in Greek, which we see about seventeen times, focuses on being made free or finding the deliverance the sinner receives. The second word, *aphiemi,* occurs much more frequently, over 140 times, and means to let go of or to send away. Essentially, these two words tell the sinner, "Be free" and tell the sin, "Be gone." See Ephesians 1:7–8. "In him we have redemption through his blood, the forgiveness of our trespasses, according to the riches of his grace, which he lavished upon us, in all wisdom and insight."

It's important to realize that this concept of forgiveness is almost completely absent from the doctrines of all man-made religions just as is the concept of God's genuine love for us. Provision is often made in these religions for working off your debt or doing sufficient good works in an attempt to balance the bad with the good. But in reality, to actually take sins away is solely a work of God. So the scribes were rightly upset to see Jesus forgiving sins in Mark 2. Little did they understand that this man, standing before them, was indeed also God incarnate. "And when Jesus saw their faith, he said to the paralytic, 'My son, your sins are forgiven.' Now some of the scribes were sitting there, questioning in their hearts, 'Why does this man speak like that? He is blaspheming! *Who can forgive sins but God alone?*'" (Mark 2:5–7, emphasis added).

Looking at this word further, we see, particularly in the Old Testament, several other words being used to give us a more complete meaning of what forgiveness means. Isaiah 55:6–7 says, "Seek the Lord while he may be found; call upon him while he is near; let the wicked forsake his way, and the unrighteous man his thoughts; let him return to the Lord, that he may have compassion on him, and to our God, for he will abundantly *pardon* (emphasis added)."

To pardon (Hebrew, *calach*, appearing forty-six times in the Old Testament) means to clear a person's record of wrongdoing before the court. Included in this meaning is the associated concept of forgiveness. How wonderful it is that God is able to do that for us because of Calvary when we confess our guilt before him.

In Colossians, we're given a phrase with a similar meaning. "And you, who were dead in your trespasses and the uncircumcision of your flesh, God made alive together with him, having forgiven us all our trespasses, by *canceling the record of debt* that stood against us with its legal demands" (Colossians 2:13, emphasis added).

Another similar word is found in Psalm 51 (Hebrew, *machah*, seen thirty-six times in the Old Testament). "Have mercy on me, O God, according to your steadfast love; according to your abundant mercy *blot out* my transgressions. Wash me thoroughly from my iniquity, and cleanse me from my sin!" (Psalm 51:1–2, emphasis added).

This word gives us the image of erasing a charge written down against us. Is it true? Can God remove the record of our evil deeds? Yes, because of the efficacy of our Lord's work at Calvary.

Another word is found in Micah 7 (Hebrew, *shalak*, appearing 125 times in the Old Testament) that means "to cast away." Micah tells his readers, "He will again have compassion on us; he will tread our iniquities under foot. You will *cast all our sins into the depths of the sea*"

(Micah 7:19, emphasis added). The idea here suggests that they would be sent to a place from which they could never be recovered, gone forever. This meaning is confirmed by the words of Hebrews 10:17, where God says, "I will remember their sins and their lawless deeds no more." While God cannot ever forget in the human sense he can chose not to remember.

It's wonderful to be forgiven by someone we have wronged. The weight is gone, just as Bunyan said, but it's better still when the relationship is restored. How much greater then is it to be forgiven by God himself? Of course, this great act of forgiving us is made possible only because of the value of the sacrifice our Lord gave at Calvary. As Hebrews 9:22 says, "Without the shedding of blood there is no forgiveness of sins." That is God's demand, yet the sacrifice must also be pure, holy, and perfect. Only the death of Jesus would suffice.

❖ SANCTIFICATION

I praise Thee, Lord for cleansing me from sin;
Fulfil Thy Word and make me pure within,
Fill me with fire, where once I burned with shame;
Grant my desire to magnify Thy name.
—J. Edwin Orr

We come now to consider our status or standing before God following our salvation, as now being "in Christ." This English word *sanctification* comes from the Latin word *sanctus*, meaning "holy." It is a core attribute of God and set also as a necessity for the Christian life.

There are two concepts necessary for an understanding of our being holy before God. First, God has saved us, and once we have accepted the sacrifice of his Son on our behalf, God now views us as holy positionally, as being "in Christ." Being "in Christ" relates to our connection or relationship to God, which is through Christ. He is our mediator and advocate, our representative before the Father on our behalf. God sees us now, in this present time, *as we shall be.* "And such were some of you. But you were washed, *you were sanctified* [made holy—a declarative statement about a past action], you were justified in the name of the Lord Jesus Christ and by the Spirit of our God" (1 Corinthians 6:11, emphasis added).

Here the emphasis is on an action God has done—we have been "made holy." In God's mind, outside the constraints of time, it is a fait accompli.

Yet in Hebrews 10:14 we move from speaking of positional holiness to practical holiness in a single verse. "For by a single offering he has perfected for all time those who are *being sanctified*" (emphasis added). Here is holiness acted out in daily life. So there is tension between a finished work, as seen in the eyes of the eternal God, and a current ongoing process within us. We see this ongoing development of God working in our lives to make us what he wants us to be in this following passage. "Therefore, my beloved, as you have always obeyed, so now, not only as in my presence but much more in my absence, *work out your own salvation* with fear and trembling, for it is God who works in you, both to will and to work for his good pleasure" (Philippians 2:12–13, emphasis added).

It's something, with the necessary help of God's Spirit, we should sincerely strive for, as the apostle Peter says. "As obedient children do not be conformed to the passions of your former ignorance, but as he who called you is holy, *you also be holy* [imperative tense—a command] in all your conduct, since it is written, 'You shall be holy, for I am holy'" (1 Peter 1:14–16, emphasis added).

What an encouragement then is to read in Ephesians that for those God foreknew would be his children, he then planned, in a past eternity, that they would be made fully holy and blameless before him. We may feel the process is slow and at times painful, understanding that it won't be fully accomplished until his coming, but the outcome is certain. We shall be changed and made holy in character and practice, which is guaranteed by the Lord himself. "Blessed be the God and Father of our Lord Jesus Christ, who has blessed us *in Christ* with every spiritual blessing in the heavenly places, even as he chose us in him [speaking of those who are *in Christ*] before the foundation of the world, *that we should be holy and blameless* before him" (Ephesians 1:3–4, emphasis added).

Also, Paul, writing to the Corinthians about Christ's return, said that at his coming we will become immortal and possess imperishable bodies, and that is possible only if the sin nature has been fully removed and we have been made holy. See this whole passage in 1 Corinthians 15.

> Behold! I tell you a mystery. We shall not all sleep, but *we shall all be changed*, in a moment, in the twinkling of an eye, at the last trumpet. For the trumpet will sound, and the dead will be raised imperishable, and we shall be changed. For this perishable body (caused by the sin nature within) must put on the imperishable, and this mortal body must put on immortality. When the perishable puts on the imperishable, and the mortal puts on immortality, then shall come to pass the saying that is written: "Death is swallowed up in victory." (1 Corinthians 15:51–54, emphasis added)

There is no death because sin is gone. And there is no sin because of the completed work of Christ within us.

The apostle Peter in his second letter writes more about this ongoing need for practical holiness in our lives when he says, "Since all these things are thus to be dissolved, *what sort of people ought you to be in lives of holiness and godliness*, waiting for and hastening the coming of the day of God" (2 Peter 3:11–12, emphasis added).

So with the help of God's Spirit, we have a job to do, and we need to put our effort into it. But there's a sure and certain hope before us. In Scripture, especially in Revelation, we see several pictures of people in "white robes," which are symbolic of their condition of purity and holiness before God. Look at the passage in Revelation 7.

> After this I looked, and behold, a great multitude that no one could number, from every nation, from all tribes and peoples and languages, standing before the throne and before the Lamb, *clothed in white robes*, with palm branches in their hands, and crying out with a loud voice, "Salvation belongs to our God who sits on the

throne, and to the Lamb!" ... [And the elder] said to me, "These are the ones coming out of the great tribulation. They have *washed their robes and made them white in the blood of the Lamb.*" (Revelation 7:9–10, 14, emphasis added)

God had made them fully holy through the sacrifice of his Son, and we also are pictured clothed in white robes of holiness and coming with the Lord at the end of the tribulation to claim his throne on earth. "And the armies of heaven, arrayed in fine linen, white and pure, were following him on white horses" (Revelation 19:14).

Let us then be fully assured that the hope of our eternal salvation, which we have already been guaranteed through the Spirit (Ephesians 1:14), is in no way dependent on this ongoing work within us of making us into the image of his Son. The benediction of Hebrews 13 requests, "Now may the God of peace ... equip you with everything good that you may do his will, working in us that which is pleasing in his sight" (vv. 20–21).

❖ Eternal Security

> When peace like a river attendeth my way,
> When sorrows like sea billows roll;
> What ever my lot, Thou hast taught me to say,
> It is well, it is well with my soul.
>
> My sin, O the bliss of this glorious thought,
> My sin, not in part but the whole,
> Is nailed to the cross and I bear it no more,
> Praise the Lord, praise the Lord, O my soul!
>
> —Horatio G. Spafford

The security of our position in Christ is directly linked to our sanctification, as we've just considered above; therefore, God, sees us as holy before him. So then Paul could ensure new believers he was writing to in his Ephesians letter that they "were sealed with the promised Holy Spirit, who is the *guarantee* of our inheritance until we acquire possession of it, to the praise of his glory" (Ephesians 1:13–14, emphasis added).

We can fully rest in God's unchanging Word. If we have doubts, then our theology is wrong; we believe that somehow we need to contribute something during our lives for God to keep his promise.

Another passage giving us real confidence is found in Romans 8. Paul says, "For I am sure that neither death nor life, nor angels nor rulers, nor things present nor things to come, nor powers, nor height nor depth, nor anything else in all creation, will be able to separate us from the love of God in Christ Jesus our Lord" (Romans 8:38–39).

Here we're told that nothing can separate us from God's love with reference to angels, rulers, or powers, and an allusion to the futility even of demonic influence to break our bond with Christ. Finally, we have the apostle John telling us at the end of his first epistle, "I write these things to you who believe in the name of the Son of God that you may know that you have eternal life" (1 John 5:13). So this eternal life is not only quantitative, meaning unending, but also qualitative life in Christ. What assurance!

Chapter Three

Salvation Stories from Scripture and a Personal Testimony

* **ABRAHAM—GENESIS 15:4–6; ROMANS 4:1–6, 11–12**

Abram was born in Ur, Mesopotamia, in a pagan Chaldean culture, probably about 1800 BC. It's likely that he spoke the Akkadian language common in that area and time. It's also possible that some of the postdiluvian patriarchs may still have been living at that time and continued to believe in and followed Yahweh. But most people had already turned from their Creator to paganism and idol worship. The dominant deity worshipped there at that time was the moon god Sin. Abram, however, responded positively when he heard the one true God speaking to him, although it was by all accounts a big ask. "Now the Lord said to Abram, 'Go from your country and your kindred and your father's house to the land that I will show you. And I will make of you a great nation'" (Genesis 12:1–2).

When he was seventy-five years old, we see that he obeyed God and left his country and people (and no doubt the idols of his father's house); he headed west, not knowing where he would end up but trusting God's promises to him. Later, when Abram was in the land of Canaan, God made a covenant (or binding agreement) with him. This covenant of blessing, which we can read in Genesis 15, was based on the fact that Abram believed God was not only the great Creator but also a promise-keeping God and would be his provider. And despite having no heir, he put his faith in him. See Genesis 15, where we read the words of almighty God again speaking to Abram,

> And behold, the word of the Lord came to him: "This man shall not be your heir; your very own son shall be your heir." And he brought him outside and said, "Look toward heaven, and number the stars, if you are able to number them." Then he said to him, "So shall your offspring be." And he believed the Lord, and *he counted it to him as righteousness.* (Genesis 15:4–6, emphasis added)

> On that day the Lord made a covenant with Abram, saying, "To your offspring I give this land, from the river of Egypt to the great river, the river Euphrates." (Genesis 15:18–19)

Although he grew up in a land that worshipped many pagan deities, Abram, whom God renamed Abraham (father of multitudes), was fully convinced that the promises given to him were from the Creator of the universe and that God was fully able to fulfill his word to him, although at that time he remained childless. He believed God, having entered into this agreement with him, would keep the promises he had obligated himself to fulfill. And Abraham's confident belief resulted in his being accepted back into a relationship with God.

The point of the story, as Paul again recounted in Romans 4, was that this "being counted righteous" happened a number of years before he was circumcised. If it had come with his act of circumcision, then it could have been seen as works, an attempt by this man to earn a right standing before God. As it was, it was a completely free gift he received because of his faith and not of any works of merit. So his right standing before God came by believing that God would keep his promises to him, as Paul concludes in Romans 4. "He received the sign of circumcision as a seal of the righteousness that he had by faith while he was still uncircumcised. The purpose was to make him the father of all who believe without being circumcised, so that righteousness would be counted to them [non-Jews] as well, and to make him the father of the circumcised who are not merely circumcised but who also walk in the footsteps of the faith that our father Abraham had before he was circumcised" (Romans 4:11–12).

Finally, Hebrews 11 confirms that Abraham lived his life by faith in God. "By faith he went to live in the land of promise, as in a foreign land, living in tents with Isaac and Jacob, heirs with him of the same promise. For he was looking forward to the city that has foundations, whose designer and builder is God" (Hebrews 11:9–10).

◆ DAVID—PSALM 32:1–5; 51:1–17

We come now to David, Israel's greatest king. Here was a man who started life as a shepherd looking after his father's sheep. And it was there on those hills that he came to understand who God was, and it was then that he put his trust in him. Much later, after he was king and his kingdom was secure, he committed a great sin before God. Here we'll consider how God dealt with him and how David responded, written as he looked back on his transgression. First, we see his repentance; and second, we see God's response.

> Have mercy on me, O God, according to your steadfast love; according to your abundant mercy blot out my transgressions. Wash me thoroughly from my iniquity, and cleanse me from my sin! For I know my transgressions, and my sin is ever before me. (Psalm 51:1–3)

> Blessed is the one whose transgression is forgiven, whose sin is covered. Blessed is the man against whom the Lord counts no iniquity, and in whose spirit there is no deceit. For when I kept silent (before he repented to the Lord), my bones wasted away through my groaning all

day long. For day and night your hand was heavy upon me; my strength was dried up as by the heat of summer. I acknowledged my sin to you, and I did not cover my iniquity; I said, "I will confess my transgressions to the Lord," and you forgave the iniquity of my sin. (Psalm 32:1–5)

This is an Old Testament story about a man of faith who fell into serious sin. David had already placed his trust in God. But now he committed this sin, culminating in a terrible crime. Was it too much? Was it beyond what God was willing to forgive? Second Samuel 11–12 details the sordid story of King David's adultery with Bathsheba, ending with the deliberate arranging of her husband's death in battle. Truly, David deserved death for this terrible transgression of God's law. Initially, it seems, however, that he thought he could get away with his deed, but even before the prophet came to him, we read that he was wracked with guilt and insomnia, as we see in Psalm 32:3–4. The prophet Nathan then confronted him with his sin, and David repented and prayed for forgiveness. Although Nathan told him God would fully forgive him, the cost or consequences of this sin would be high. He was the king and in a position that influenced many people, making his sin that much more serious. He was told that the child created by this liaison would die; in addition, there would be bitter feuding within his household for the rest of his life. David accepted this news as from the Lord. Indeed, he would have accepted almost any discipline that would allow him to once again be restored to fellowship with the God he loved.

David details his sin and the painful journey back to God in those two poems, as recorded in Psalms 51 and 32. They start as every salvation story should, with an acknowledgment of his sin and that it was too great for him ever to fix himself. But then he writes of throwing himself on the mercy of God for forgiveness. He understood the problem, just as the scribes and Pharisees mentioned previously knew in Jesus's day when they said, "Who can forgive sins but God alone?" (Luke 5:21). But in reality our holy God, also being a God of love, delights to forgive sin, even great sin, when people come to him in true repentance.

So was his sin fully forgiven? Was he fully restored to fellowship with God? We find the answer in the amazing covenant promise God gave to David at the end of his life in 2 Samuel 7:12–19.

> "When your days are fulfilled and you lie down with your fathers, I will raise up your offspring after you, who shall come from your body, and I will establish his kingdom. He shall build a house for my name, and I will establish the throne of his kingdom forever. I will be to him a father, and he shall be to me a son. When he commits iniquity, I will discipline him with the rod of men, with the stripes of the sons of men, but my steadfast love will not depart from him, as I took it from Saul, whom I put away from before you. And your house and your kingdom shall be made sure forever before me. Your throne shall be established forever." In accordance with all these words, and in accordance with all this vision, Nathan spoke to David. Then King David went in and sat before the Lord and said, "Who am I, O Lord God, and what is my house, that you have brought me thus far?"

The amazing thing is that David's sin was never mentioned as God made this covenant with him. The greatness of God's blessing to David overwhelmed him. This is a lesson to us; we must never underestimate God's ability to forgive even the worst of sinners when a person comes to him in true repentance, sorrow, and faith. Yes, some consequences came as a result of his sin, but his fellowship with God was restored.

❖ Zacchaeus—Luke 19:1–10

Moving to the New Testament, we come to the story of Zacchaeus. Unlike David, here's a man we might consider unlikely to even be interested in seeking and desiring to find forgiveness from God. Read the story in Luke 19.

[Jesus] entered Jericho and was passing through. And there was a man named Zacchaeus. He was a chief tax collector and was rich. And he was seeking to see who Jesus was, but on account of the crowd he could not, because he was small of stature. So, he ran on ahead and climbed up into a sycamore tree to see him, for he was about to pass that way. And when Jesus came to the place, he looked up and said to him, "Zacchaeus, hurry and come down, for I must stay at your house today." So, he hurried and came down and received him joyfully. And when they saw it, they all grumbled, "He has gone in to be the guest of a man who is a sinner." And Zacchaeus stood and said to the Lord [a public confession], "Behold, Lord, the half of my goods I give to the poor. And if I have defrauded anyone of anything, I restore it fourfold." (Luke 19:1–8)

The first information Luke gives us about this man is that he was rich and had a prominent position as the chief tax man of the region on behalf of the hated Romans. No doubt he dressed appropriately in finely made robes. The second thing we're told is that he desired to see Jesus but was hindered by his short stature. What a surprise to us that he would be interested in seeing Jesus. But it's evident that this wasn't just a casual passing interest, for he was willing to put aside his dignity and any other concerns about how this would look for a man of his wealth and position as he ran ahead of the crowd and, overcoming his handicap, climbed up into a tree, of all places, to see him. The people without a doubt knew what kind of a man he was; he was working for the Romans and accumulating his wealth by skimming tax money from the people.

But when Jesus stopped beneath the tree that day and told him to come down so they could dine together, he immediately hurried down; and then the text says, "And received him [Jesus] joyfully." And then it records him saying in verse 8, "Behold, Lord, the half of my goods I give to the poor. And if I have defrauded anyone of anything, I restore it fourfold" (Luke 19:8). Immediately Jesus responded by saying, "Today salvation has come to this house, since he also is a son of Abraham. For the Son of Man came to seek and to save the lost" (Luke 19:9–10).

This indeed is what salvation is all about. Zacchaeus knew he was hopelessly lost and needed God's intervention. Read what John says in his Gospel about who could receive this salvation. "He came to his own, and his own people did not receive him. But to *all who did receive him,* who believed in his name, he gave the right to become children of God" (John 1:11–12, emphasis added).

As with salvation in general, the proof is immediately seen in Zacchaeus's changed heart and life. Now the money that had been his total focus and his god meant nothing compared to what and whom he had just received. When faith follows conviction and repentance, there will inevitably be real change in a life.

❖ CORNELIUS THE CENTURION—ACTS 10:1–48

Another instructive story comes to us, as Luke recorded, concerning the time when God used Peter to reach out to the Gentiles through Cornelius, a just man and a seeker of God. In Acts 10:1–6, 25–33, we read,

> At Caesarea there was a man named Cornelius, a centurion of what was known as the Italian Cohort, a devout man who feared God with all his household, gave alms generously to the people, and prayed continually to God. About the ninth hour of the day he saw clearly in a vision an angel of God come in and say to him, "Cornelius." And he stared at him in terror and said, "What is it, Lord?" And he said to him, "Your prayers and your alms have ascended as a memorial before God. And now send men to Joppa and bring one Simon who is called Peter" … When Peter entered, Cornelius met him and fell down at his feet and worshiped him. But Peter lifted him up, saying, "Stand up; I too am a man." And as he talked with him, he went in and found many

persons gathered. And he said to them, "You yourselves know how unlawful it is for a Jew to associate with or to visit anyone of another nation, but God has shown me that I should not call any person common or unclean. So when I was sent for, I came without objection. I ask then why you sent for me." And Cornelius said, "Four days ago, about this hour, I was praying in my house at the ninth hour, and behold, a man stood before me in bright clothing and said, 'Cornelius, your prayer has been heard and your alms have been remembered before God. Send therefore to Joppa and ask for Simon who is called Peter. He is lodging in the house of Simon, a tanner, by the sea.' So I sent for you at once, and you have been kind enough to come. Now therefore we are all here in the presence of God to hear all that you have been commanded by the Lord."

Peter then presented the gospel message to all those gathered. He spoke of Jesus and who he was and about his death at Calvary and his resurrection. Peter ended the message by telling them that forgiveness of sins was now available to all who were willing to put their faith in him. The story concludes with the following scene, starting at verse 44,

> While Peter was still saying these things, the Holy Spirit fell on all who heard the word. And the believers from among the circumcised who had come with Peter were amazed, because the gift of the Holy Spirit was poured out even on the Gentiles. For they were hearing them speaking in tongues and extolling God. Then Peter declared, "Can anyone withhold water for baptizing these people, who have received the Holy Spirit just as we have?" And he commanded them to be baptized in the name of Jesus Christ. Then they asked him to remain for some days. (Acts 10:44–48)

This is the wonderful story of the good news of salvation first being proclaimed to someone who wasn't Jewish. It came by Peter to Cornelius and his family and friends, a man characterized as being a "devout man" and "one who feared God."

Certainly, he was a man who was no longer a pagan, like so many Romans of the time, but he was someone who believed Jehovah, spoken of in the Jewish Old Testament, was in fact the Creator God, to whom all worship was due. His devotion to God was expressed by his regularly praying and generously giving tithing money to the Jewish people, among whom he was living. While these deeds could in no way save him, it says in our story that God took note of them. It has been said that a seeking sinner and the seeking Savior will always meet.

What it doesn't say here is that because of his conscientious religious activity, he was therefore already in a right standing before God with his sins forgiven. But he had in sincerity opened his heart to seek the truth, and God for his part would ensure that he found it. The passage records that Cornelius said, "Now therefore we are all here in the presence of God to hear all that you have been commanded by the Lord" (Acts 10:33). Here indeed was a seeker ready to hear the message from God and act on it.

Peter attested to having been an eyewitness of these things and that he had been called by God to testify of these things. Finally, he spoke to them of Jesus, telling them that he was the one who would be the judge at the end of time—and most importantly, that it was through him and through believing in him (or receiving him or making a decision to follow him) that people could receive forgiveness of their sins.

These people were so ready to do this that Peter's sermon was disrupted as the people began believing and then as the Holy Spirit came on them, and they began speaking in tongues and praising God. The result was that they were baptized, at that very time becoming a part of the church, just as had earlier happened to the newly saved Jewish believers at Pentecost. So with that auspicious beginning, the gospel was now to be proclaimed to all peoples of the world. As Paul says in Ephesians, Jesus "might reconcile us both [Jew and Gentile] to God in one body through the cross" (2:16).

These people heard the gospel that day and received it as the truth of

God and put their faith in Jesus as Savior. Now, redeemed by his blood, they were indwelt by his Spirit and baptized by those who had come with Peter. What a celebration of joy must have occurred that day!

❖ THE PHILIPPIAN JAILER—ACTS 16:22–34

Lastly, we come to the story of a man who was likely a pagan man, and yet again we see him coming to faith in Christ. It is the conversion story of an official in the Gentile city of Philippi, who turned from being a follower of pagan religion to being a follower of the resurrected Lord Jesus Christ. The story starts with Paul and Silas being attacked by an angry crowd, as instigated by the officials.

> The crowd joined in attacking them, and the magistrates tore the garments off them and gave orders to beat them with rods. And when they had inflicted many blows upon them, they threw them into prison, ordering the jailer to keep them safely. Having received this order, he put them into the inner prison and fastened their feet in the stocks.
>
> About midnight Paul and Silas were praying and singing hymns to God, and the prisoners were listening to them, and suddenly there was a great earthquake, so that the foundations of the prison were shaken. And immediately all the doors were opened, and everyone's bonds were unfastened. When the jailer woke and saw that the prison doors were open, he drew his sword and was about to kill himself, supposing that the prisoners had escaped. But Paul cried with a loud voice, "Do not harm yourself, for we are all here." And the jailer called for lights and rushed in and trembling with fear he fell down before Paul and Silas. Then he brought them out and said, "Sirs, what must I do to be saved?" And they said, "Believe in the Lord Jesus, and you will be saved, you and your household." And they spoke the word of

the Lord to him and to all who were in his house And
he took them the same hour of the night and washed
their wounds; and he was baptized at once, he and all his
family. Then he brought them up into his house and set
food before them. And he rejoiced along with his entire
household that he had believed in God. (Acts 16:22–34)

No doubt this jailer may have already been feeling pangs of guilt
because of his participation in the abuse given to these two missionaries,
particularly in light of their response to their beating by showing such
resolve and singing praises to God. Then the miraculous earthquake
happened that opened every door and lock in the jail. According to
Roman law, the jailer's life would be forfeit for every prisoner who
escaped, so the man was terrified and thought he'd rather just kill
himself first.

Paul knew this and quickly intervened, assuring him that all the
prisoners were accounted for, and no one had tried to escape. The jailer
then brought Paul and Silas out and said, "Sirs, what must I do to be
saved?" (v. 30). What triggered this question? Without a doubt, it must
have been that he had heard the good news of Jesus from them earlier,
but now, convicted of his sins, his heart was opened to receive the
truth of the gospel message. Paul gave the simple but profound answer:
"Believe in the Lord Jesus, and you will be saved" (v. 31).

As we read the rest of the story, we find that Paul had the opportunity
to tell the gospel message to his whole household. The passage ends by
saying that "all heard and received the gospel" (v. 32), that "all were
baptised" (v. 33) that very night, and that "all rejoiced" together (v. 34)—
conviction and repentance followed by faith. That's the way of salvation.

❖ A Personal Testimony

Indulge me by allowing a personal story of my own salvation. I had the
privilege of being raised in a Christian home and was faithfully taken
to meetings at our small Christian assembly from a very young age,
probably starting with Sunday school at about three. I was fascinated

by all the great stories and real-life adventures in the Bible filled with heroism and sometimes wars and even death.

Besides Sunday school, there were the gospel meeting each Sunday evening and the gospel tent series almost every summer. I look back with fond memories of being with these believers, who evidently loved me and cared for my spiritual welfare. Here we heard about our sin, about being unfit for heaven because of it, and about the reality of hell and the certainty of it for those not saved; yet there was the truth of God's love to us through the death of his Son. Logically then, I thought, if God, Creator of all, was truly holy and loving, this redemption story made sense to me. So at an early age, I began thinking, like the Philippian jailer, *What must I do to be saved?* There were many New Testament verses used to tell us clearly what we are to do—"Believe!" Take the greatest of them all. "For God so loved the world, that he gave his only Son, that whoever *believes* in him should not perish but have eternal life" (John 3:16, emphasis added).

Yet I couldn't honestly remember a time when I didn't believe the truth of the gospel. This was God's Word, and what he said was true. So what was I to do? I certainly didn't count myself as one of the saved. And so I stumbled over this word *believe*. Nothing I heard seemed to clear up my dilemma.

In our particular Christian assembly, as I was growing up, there was another tradition, starting on the first Sunday of January each new year. Men of the assembly got up each Sunday evening to give their testimony and talk about how God had saved them. This event continued until they had all taken their turn. I loved listening to their stories and not just because I liked stories, although I did. No, I was listening to see what a person like me did to be saved. I closely followed along as they experienced conviction of their sin and as they struggled with understanding God's salvation. But then, it seemed, they had suddenly understood and with great happiness exclaimed they were saved and had peace with God. And I wondered, *What did I just miss?* I believed in God. I also believed I was a sinner, and my parents assisted in this understanding. I believed Jesus was indeed God's Son come into this world and that he had died on the cross at Calvary, paying the penalty for our sins. And I believed he rose from the dead and was alive. And yet I remained on the outside looking in, perhaps thinking there must be a special kind of belief that saved.

When I was nine or ten, there were gospel tent meetings nearby that carried on for several weeks each of those summers in 1958 and 1959. Many of the teenagers, a little older than I, were saved during that time. I even stayed behind one night to talk to the preacher, but while agreeing to all the questions he asked about my understanding of salvation and listening to him read verses from the Bible, I was left not knowing what to do next. It seemed much the same the next winter during another series of gospel meetings in March 1960. One night after the meeting, the preacher asked whether I would like to talk with him. He read a number of gospel verses to me, finally coming to John 6:47, which in the KJV, which we all used at that time, says, "Verily, verily, I say unto you, He that believeth on me hath everlasting life" (John 6:47).

Then he asked me, "Do you believe?" I think I could see where he was heading with the question, but after some hesitation, I said yes, since I did believe it was true, and he smiled and shook my hand. I was a little unsure that it could be that simple. I had doubts. I think when my Sunday school teacher later asked how I knew I was saved, I assured him by saying the preacher had said so. What he might have done, I'm thinking now many years later, was ask me whether I'd like to pray and thank the Lord for this gift of salvation. So I went along for a time in a state of uncertainly, but then later as a more mature eleven-year-old, sitting in another meeting and listening again to the gospel message, in my uncertainty I simply prayed to God and said in my silent prayer, "Whether I accepted Jesus as my Savior before or not, I accept him now, tonight." I thanked God for his salvation, and my doubts were settled as I rested on God's salvation for me.

The process didn't need to be that difficult. But I suppose at that time there seemed to be too many young people coming home from summer Bible camps with professions after having repeated a formulaic salvation prayer. Little changed in their lives as proof of salvation, and there were concerns about the lack of understanding of what they had done and possible lack of repentance, leaving them living in false hope and still in their sins. So evangelists, especially those associated with the Brethren movement backed off on coaching or guiding a person into something artificial, waiting for the Spirit to open a person's eyes. Often this resulted in the person reaching a point of desperation and resignation, of starting to believe he or she would never be saved, that he or she was destined for hell until at last he or she just rested in the Lord's finished work.

For me, however, the missing piece was found in John 1:12, quoted earlier. "But to all *who did receive him*, who believed in his name, he gave the right to become children of God" (emphasis added). Here is an active faith *reaching out* to receive the gift so freely offered. This isn't a kind of work that contributes to our salvation but acceptance by faith of the finished work of Christ. We see something similar in the verse my grandmother read to my father when he was saved as a young boy. "*If you confess* with your mouth that Jesus is Lord and believe in your heart that God raised him from the dead, you will be saved" (Romans 10:9, emphasis added).

Confessing Jesus as Savior is evidence of that step of faith. Baptism as well, though not able to save us, is another outward act giving evidence of an inner heart change that testifies to others. The best evidence by far is a changed life, one lived for the Lord Jesus. Since then, the Lord has given me a desire and some opportunity to serve him. It's been a joy to do so for this One who so graciously saved me.

Chapter Four

Foundations of the Biblical Theology of Salvation

❖ Who God Is: The Nature of Our Eternal Creator God

In his essential being, God is the eternal, self-existent, almighty One who yet subsists in three persons—Father, Son, and Holy Spirit, the Trinity. He has many attributes to which we could never attain or even fully comprehend such as his omniscience, omnipresence, omnipotence, and eternal existence. But in particular, it is the character of his person that is so glorious—infinite in holiness, love, and wisdom. As Exodus 15:11 says, "Who is like you, majestic in holiness." He is therefore perfect in all his ways, always acting righteously in accordance with his holy, unchanging character. He never reneges on a promise or goes back on his word or ever acts in any way but that which aligns with his unchanging character. Because of his perfect holiness, he hates sin, yet at the same time he is truly a God of love. And that love was expressed in his goodness to us. He planned a salvation that included God the Son coming into this world as fully human so that, as we read in Hebrews 2, he could die for us and defeat Satan. Being the perfect human, he was able to willingly offer himself for our salvation. And yet in his perfect wisdom, at the same time he was able to remain eternal God. Therefore, through death, he could make a sacrifice of infinite worth that all might come and be saved. One of the best summaries of this salvation in all Scripture is found in Paul's Roman epistle, as previously quoted.

> For all have sinned and fall short of the glory of God, and are justified by his grace as a gift, through the redemption that is in Christ Jesus, whom God put forward as a propitiation (a satisfaction for his holiness) by his blood, to be received by faith. This was to show God's righteousness, because in his divine forbearance he had passed over [temporarily covered over] former sins. It was to show his righteousness at the present time, so that he might be *just and the justifier of the one who has faith in Jesus.* (Romans 3:23–26, emphasis added)

This passage sums up for us how through his redemptive plan we are able to experience forgiveness of sins and therefore come once again into the presence of his holiness (Exodus 15:11), all because of the great love with which he loved us (Ephesians 2:4), receiving us back to himself.

In his great wisdom then, he created a plan of redemption, displaying his infinite love, yet without any compromise of his great and awesome holiness.

❖ Who We Are—Human Beings Created in God's Image

As human beings, God has uniquely made us in his own image, so our Creator continues to see us as of great value to himself. And despite the fall, we still carry the imprint of his creation within us. Unlike the rest of this earthly creation, we have an eternal spirit within us given from God and therefore a God-consciousness, self-awareness, and moral consciousness. And unlike all other creatures in this world, we have free will, an ability to choose our course in this world and to choose whether we will live in dependence on God or in independence and rebellion against God. After the flood, God spoke to Noah, as we see in Genesis 9, and emphasized the value or worth he continued to put on us as human beings despite our sin. He proclaimed the death penalty for deliberately taking another's life. Hear God's words: "And for your lifeblood I will require a reckoning: from every beast I will require it and from man. From his fellow man I will require a reckoning for the life of man. 'Whoever sheds the blood of man, by man shall his blood be shed, for God made man in his own image'" (Genesis 9:5–6).

Referencing this eternal spirit mentioned above, which makes us unique from all other living things, we see the preacher telling us in Ecclesiastes, "Man is going to his eternal home, ... the dust returns to the earth as it was, and the spirit returns to God who gave it" (Ecclesiastes 12:5, 7). As long or brief as our time is physically on this earth, Scripture confirms that our souls will live on. So God creates us with intrinsic worth based on our attributes as being created in his image. This pertains to everyone no manner the race or gender or whether the person is rich or poor or healthy or disabled, young or old. Nothing can change this fact, and it should directly impact the way we treat one another as human beings. We are, all of us, God's special creation. This must include not only our friends but also our enemies as well as infants and the elderly and disabled. Worth cannot be based on the productivity of people's lives or even their cognitive awareness. Abortion and euthanasia then are clearly sin, abominations to the Lord. In the end, we will all give an account to our God for how we have treated one another.

Today it seems that our society is doing its best to blur the lines and distinctiveness between animals and people. People who have a pet are no longer called their "owner" but their "mommy" or "daddy." And the organization PETA (People for the Ethical Treatment of Animals) is no longer really trying to get us to treat animals more *humanely* but more *humanly*—to elevate their intrinsic value to be more equal to people as founded on an evolutionary worldview. After all, are not human beings simply a higher order of species in the phylogenetic tree?

Going back to Scripture, we see in Hebrews 2 that the writer is speaking of the incarnation of the Lord. There he places mankind just a little lower than angels, with the rest of creation in subjection to us. "What is man, that you are mindful of him, or the son of man, that you care for him? You made him for a little while lower than the angels; you have crowned him with glory and honor, putting everything in subjection under his feet" (Hebrews 2:6–8).

We must then as Christians value and respect people, no matter who, as unique and made in the image of God. And we need to practically live this truth out day by day in how we treat one another.

◆ WHO WE ARE—HUMAN BEINGS CREATED IN GOD'S IMAGE BUT FALLEN

Scripture tells us we are fallen. This refers to our separation from fellowship with God, which at the beginning existed in the Garden of Eden. It came because of an act of rebellion in the garden, resulting in disastrous consequences. We are now fallen from that special position of closeness because of our sin nature, and this results in our propensity to sin. Being fallen and cut off from that fellowship, we are now unable to live righteously, and in fact in our natural state, we are held captive to our sin nature (Romans 6:12–14) and are unable *not* to sin.

Yet there remains within us human beings a longing to have that relationship restored. After all, we were made for that. That is why religions of every stripe are so pervasive in every part of the world as people invent ways to try to find their way back to God. Yet in this fallen state and because of the sin nature within us, we are incapable of doing any works of righteousness that would be acceptable to God in restoring that lost relationship. "And you were dead in the trespasses and sins in which you once walked, following the course of this world, following the prince of the power of the air, the spirit that is now at work in the sons of disobedience—among whom we all once lived in the passions of our flesh, carrying out the desires of the body and the mind, and were by nature children of wrath, like the rest of mankind" (Ephesians 2:1–3).

We also see that truth after Adam sinned in the garden, and although he was already separated spiritually from God by this action, he wasn't dead in the sense that he was completely insensitive to or cut off from an awareness of God, unable to communicate with God, or oblivious to an understanding of morality. He didn't lose his ability to choose his course in life.

God came to him, talked to him, and held both him and Eve responsible for their actions. And further, he gave them a glimpse of what the future was now to hold for them. Then in grace he provided skins for them to clothe their nakedness and a promise of future salvation.

❖ WHO WE ARE—THE REMNANTS OF OUR SPECIAL CREATION, FALLEN YET STILL HUMAN

Though fallen, we remain sentient, rational, freewill moral human beings made in the image of God with a God-given eternally existent spirit within us. And so we have a consciousness of God, his holiness, and eternity; but we also have a consciousness of our sin separating us from him. Since we then have this awareness of the eternal and a knowledge of true righteousness, the Holy Spirit is able to work in each heart to convict us, to draw us back to God, who loves us. As we respond to that, we will be progressively given a clearer understanding of our need and helplessness and of the salvation he has prepared for us. Ecclesiastes 3:11 says, "He has put eternity into man's heart," so we innately know we aren't like animals; we were made for a relationship with deity. Also, Paul tells us in Romans 1 that in our hearts we know God exists, yet in our rebellion, we try to deny what is so self-evident.

"For the wrath of God is revealed from heaven against all ungodliness and unrighteousness of men, who by their unrighteousness *suppress the truth*. For what can be known about God is plain to them, because God has shown it to them. For his invisible attributes, namely, his eternal power and divine nature, have been *clearly perceived*, ever since the creation of the world, in the things that have been made. So they are without excuse" (Romans 1:18–20, emphasis added).

That's why the psalmist could write in Psalm 14:1, "The fool says in his heart, 'There is no God.'" Looking around at our world and all creation and even within ourselves, Paul says, it's plain to see the reality of our Maker.

God *is* in the infinity of his eternal being, so with the spirit God gave within us, we are also forced to see the reality of our sin nature, which Paul says causes us to "fall short of the glory of God." If there was no God, there would, as a consequence, be no consciousness of sin. Read what Paul writes about this. "For when Gentiles, who do not have the law, by nature do what the law requires, they are a law to themselves, even though they do not have the law. They show that *the work of the law is written on their hearts*, while their conscience also bears witness" (Romans 2:14–15, emphasis added).

◆ Who Jesus Is—Eternally God the Son Yet Fully Incarnate in Our Humanity

There are so many Scriptures that reveal to us the truth of who Jesus was and is that it's difficult to choose which to use here. These were chosen since they clearly show Jesus to be both the promised Messiah and also very God becoming truly human. Isaiah says, "For to us *a child is born*, to us a son is given; and the government shall be upon his shoulder, and his name shall be called Wonderful Counselor, *Mighty God, Everlasting Father*, Prince of Peace. Of the increase of his government and of peace there will be no end, on *the throne of David* and over his kingdom, to establish it and to uphold it with justice and with righteousness from this time forth and forevermore" (Isaiah 9:6–7, emphasis added).

This prophecy given to Isaiah speaks of the coming Messiah who is to be born yet also uses terms of deity, such as "Mighty God, Everlasting Father," so it reveals to them who Messiah would really be. As a man he was born as every other human being and is to inherit the throne of David as Israel's future king. As God, he will bring everlasting peace, justice, and righteousness.

This next passage in Matthew's Gospel confirms Jesus was to be the Messiah because of the name Jesus, which he was to be given; the name means "Jehovah saves." But then the angel also quotes to Joseph the amazing words found in Isaiah 7 that he is also to be Immanuel, meaning, "God with us." See the words the angel spoke to Joseph. "'Joseph, son of David, do not fear to take Mary as your wife, for that which is conceived in her is from the Holy Spirit. She will bear a son, and you shall call his name *Jesus*, for he will save his people from their sins.' All this took place to fulfill what the Lord had spoken by the prophet: 'Behold, the virgin shall conceive and bear a son, and they shall call his name *Immanuel*' (which means, God with us)" (Matthew 1:20–23, emphasis added).

The apostle John also confirms this truth at the beginning of his Gospel when he identifies Jesus as the eternal Word, predating even his coming into the world, and then says plainly that the Word is God. "In the beginning [when the beginning of Creation began] was the Word, and the Word was with God, and *the Word was God*" (John 1:1, emphasis added).

In the Epistle to the Colossians below, Paul says that the Lord was the creator of "all things." And then further tells us that "in him all things hold together." He is, in fact, the controller of the elemental forces that hold our universe and world together, giving it stability.

> He is the image of the invisible God, the firstborn of all creation. For *by him all things were created*, in heaven and on earth, visible and invisible, whether thrones or dominions or rulers or authorities—all things were created through him and for him. And *he is before all things, and in him all things hold together*. And he is the head of the body, the church. He is the beginning, the firstborn from the dead, that in everything he might be preeminent. For *in him all the fullness of God was pleased to dwell*, and through him to reconcile to himself all things, whether on earth or in heaven, making peace by the blood of his cross. (Colossians 1:15–20, emphasis added)

Finally, in Revelation we see this great proclamation of the Lord himself. "'I am the Alpha and the Omega,' says the Lord God, 'who is and who was and who is to come, the Almighty [Sovereign Lord]'" (Revelation 1:8).

Theologians have struggled with this novel concept of how Jesus could be both fully man and so, as Scripture says in Hebrews 2, was able to die for us yet at the same time remain fully eternal God. This hypostasis of two natures in one person was something the early church struggled with. The Nicene Creed, largely drafted by Athanasius in AD

(Anno Domini, in the year of our Lord) 325 at the first church council, sought to give clarity to this belief and in part said, "We believe in one God, the Father Almighty, Maker of *heaven* and earth, and of all things visible and invisible. And in one Lord Jesus Christ, the only-begotten Son of God, begotten of the Father 'before all worlds,' Light of Light, very God of very God, begotten, not made, consubstantial with the Father; By whom all things were made [both in heaven and on earth]; who for us men, and for our salvation, came down from heaven, and was incarnate by the Holy Ghost and of the Virgin Mary, and was made man."[9]

From this came the affirmation that our Lord existed from eternity past, as John 1:1 tells us, and yet also consisted from his incarnation of two natures within one person. So God the Son didn't simply appear as a man although not being truly human; nor as God did he just inhabit the body of a real human being, Jesus, while in essence remaining only God. Instead, in the infinite wisdom of deity, he became a new entity, being both God and man in one complete and perfect person. While as God, he upholds the universe by the word of his power, yet as Jesus he could become tired and hungry and certainly feel pain.

Lastly, we are told that Jesus Christ, having come into the world to save us, is even now building his kingdom, composed of all those who from the very beginning have put their trust in him. The signs given us in Scripture affirm that very soon he will physically return to earth as sovereign over all to reign eternally as King of kings and Lord of lords. How wonderful that we believers can become part of that kingdom even now and live in the anticipation of its soon coming fulfillment!

❖ THE COSMIC BATTLE LINES DRAWN

God desires us as human beings to be reconciled to him, but Satan, the great deceiver, works hard in this world to thwart God's plans, blind mankind, and occupy us in our pursuits. He also has our sin nature to help him in this task as well as using the world system in which we live to entice us. Scripture aptly calls him "the god of this world."

> And even if our gospel is veiled, it is veiled only to those who are perishing. In their case *the god of this world* has blinded the minds of the unbelievers, to keep them from seeing the light of the gospel of the glory of Christ, who is the image of God. For what we proclaim is not ourselves, but Jesus Christ as Lord, with ourselves as your servants for Jesus' sake. For God, who said, "Let light shine out of darkness," has shone in our hearts to give the light of the knowledge of the glory of God in the face of Jesus Christ. (2 Corinthians 4:4–6, emphasis added)

Here we see Paul writing of this very real fight between good and evil for the souls of men. Yet despite Satan's power and the darkness in which he surrounds us, Paul tells us the light of God through his Spirit has pierced the darkness, bringing light. And John tells us that the light of Christ and his Spirit are stronger. John 1:5 says, "The light [of Jesus Christ] shines in the darkness, and the darkness has not overcome it [or conquered it]."

In the end, despite Satan's power, lies, and attempts to keep us under his control, God gives us the responsibility to choose to remain in that state or to turn to Christ. This momentous decision belongs with each person individually. Luke also writes of the scene in heaven when someone accepts the Lord, "I tell you, there is joy before the angels of God over one sinner who repents" (Luke 15:10). John speaks of Jesus being that light come into the world to save us and our responsibility to receive him. John tells us, "*The true light, which enlightens everyone*, was coming into the world. He was in the world, and the world was made through him, yet the world did not know him. He came to his own, and his own people did not receive him. But to *all who did receive him*, who believed in his name, he gave the right to become children of God, who were born, not of blood nor of the will of the flesh nor of the will of man, but of God" (John 1:9–13, emphasis added).

Yet Scripture tells us clearly that as free choice agents it's possible to resist God's will in the matter of salvation. We read of the Jewish leaders' response above at his first coming, and later Paul tells of others at the end of this age at the coming of the Antichrist. Listen to the words first of Jesus and then of Paul.

> "O Jerusalem, Jerusalem, the city that kills the prophets and stones those who are sent to it! How often would I have gathered your children together as a hen gathers her brood under her wings, and *you would not!*" (Matthew 23:37, emphasis added)

> The coming of the lawless one is by the activity of Satan with all power and false signs and wonders, and with all wicked deception for those who are perishing, because *they refused to love the truth and so be saved.* (2 Thessalonians 2:9–10, emphasis added)

However, despite the wicked deception talked about above, God's Word says that people, even at that time, will still have sufficient light to turn to the Lord or to knowingly turn away from the truth and suffer the consequences of their choice.

✦ SALVATION, WHOLLY OF GOD

Salvation, with sins forgiven and being reconciled to God or being made right with him, is a great gift given by his grace, and it's wholly a miracle of God. Receiving the gift of salvation is a personal choice offered to each individual and is received by faith. But the transaction of salvation itself is wholly of God. Because of the provision at Calvary made by Christ, the Son of God, salvation from our sins and reconciliation to God have been made available to us. At that moment of faith, the individual's sins are judiciously forgiven, and he or she is made a child of God and received or adopted into his family. In addition, we are indwelt and sealed by his Spirit (see Romans 8:9–11) and given the sure promise of an eternal inheritance.

Listen how Paul opens his great opus on the gospel to the Roman believers. "Paul, a servant of Christ Jesus, called to be an apostle, set apart for the *gospel of God* [its author], which he promised beforehand through his prophets in the holy Scriptures, *concerning his Son* [its procurer] who was descended from David according to the flesh and was declared to be the Son of God in power according to *the Spirit of holiness* [through whom it is made active] by his resurrection from the dead, Jesus Christ our Lord" (Romans 1:1–4, emphasis added).

Paul calls the good news he proclaimed the "gospel of God" due to its origin in the mind of our loving God and "concerning his Son" because it was, in fact, God the Son who came into our world, taking on our humanity. And as the God-man, he was the One able to provide this salvation for us through his human death and then by rising from the dead through his resurrection. In addition, he has given to the Spirit the double tasks of first calling people to himself (John 16: 8–11) and then completing the work of salvation in us, as Paul says in his letter to the Ephesians, "until we all attain to the unity of the faith and of the knowledge of the Son of God, to mature manhood, to the measure of the stature of the fullness of Christ" (Ephesians 4:13).

❖ WHO WE ARE AS CHRISTIANS—HUMAN BEINGS CREATED IN GOD'S IMAGE, FALLEN YET FORGIVEN

As human beings and though sinners, people retain the moral capacity to understand our unfitness to be in God's presence. We also, as spiritual beings, can be convinced of our sin and drawn to the Savior through the work of the Spirit of God. Finally, God has commanded us to repent and turn to him for salvation. We have free will to choose to reject or accept this invitation. By accepting it, we are fully forgiven and reconciled to God and brought into his family.

> And you, who were dead in your trespasses and the uncircumcision of your flesh, God made alive together with him, *having forgiven us all our trespasses, by canceling the record of debt that stood against us with its legal demands.* This he set aside, nailing it to the cross [of Calvary]. He disarmed the rulers and authorities and put them to open shame, by triumphing over them

in him [through his resurrection]. (Colossians 2:13–15, emphasis added)

And he commanded us to preach to the people and to testify that he is the one appointed by God to be judge of the living and the dead. To him all the prophets bear witness that *everyone who believes in him receives forgiveness of sins through his name.* (Acts 10:42–43, emphasis added)

Now, having been reconciled and made spiritually alive to God and empowered by the Holy Spirit, we are called to be ambassadors for the Lord in this world. "Therefore, if anyone is in Christ, he is a new creation. The old has passed away; behold, the new has come. All this is from God, who through Christ reconciled us to himself and gave us the ministry of reconciliation" (2 Corinthians 5:17–18).

❖ WHO WE ARE AS BEING "IN CHRIST"—FORGIVEN AND NOW ADOPTED INTO HIS FAMILY

Lastly, having been saved and forgiven, we are now also eternally secure in this new relationship of being a part of his family and having the assurance of this from God's Word. On receiving eternal life, our eyes are opened to eternal realities, and we can often see the Lord working and leading in our lives. Yet it's wonderful that this certainty is based not on how we feel at any given moment but on his eternal, unchanging character, his promises, and his immutable Word. See these words from God by the apostles John and Paul about our new life in Christ. First, John quotes Jesus, who is speaking about our salvation, in which he gave us a double guarantee. "My sheep hear my voice, and I know them, and they follow me. I give them eternal life, and they will never perish, and no one will snatch them out of my hand. My Father, who has given them to me, is greater than all, and no one is able to snatch them out of the Father's hand. I and the Father are one" (John 10:27–30).

Then Paul tells us in Romans 8 that if we are believers, the Holy

Spirit dwells within us, adopting us into his family and with that, pronouncing us both children and heirs of God. "You have received the Spirit of *adoption as sons*, by whom we cry, 'Abba! Father!' The Spirit himself bears witness with our spirit that we are *children of God*, and if children, then *heirs*—heirs of God and fellow heirs with Christ" (Romans 8:15–17, emphasis added).

Similarly, in the opening verses of Ephesians, Paul exults in the knowledge of God's plans for us who believe. "Blessed be the God and Father of our Lord Jesus Christ, who has blessed us in Christ with every spiritual blessing in the heavenly places, even as he chose us in him before the foundation of the world, that we [those who are "in Christ," i.e., believers] should be holy and blameless before him. In love he predestined us for *adoption through Jesus Christ*, according to the purpose of his will" (Ephesians 1:3–5, emphasis added).

These verses all focus on God's plans for those who are "in Christ," for those who have trusted the Lord Jesus as their Savior. All these have already been adopted into his family. None will be abandoned or left out of his plans. And in a coming day, each believer will come to experience a state of perfect holiness and be made blameless, enjoying unblemished fellowship with God. Then finally in verses 13–14 of that wonderful first chapter of this epistle, he tells us that the indwelling Spirit is the guarantee, the security, of that eternal inheritance. "When you heard the word of truth, the gospel of your salvation, and believed in him, [you] were sealed with the promised Holy Spirit, who is *the guarantee of our inheritance* until we acquire possession of it, to the praise of his glory" (Ephesians 1:13–14, emphasis added).

But what about those people who claim Christ as Savior but later turn from the truth? In those cases, I believe we are looking at two groups of people. First, we see those who were never saved, never having been reconciled to God, but were mere professors bearing no fruit.

Second, we see those who have been saved but moved away from close fellowship with the Father. They have slid back, allowing Satan to ensnare them and take back some degree of control in their lives. In the first category, we see Judas Iscariot, who, though one of the disciples for nearly three years, was never a true believer in Jesus. The apostle John mentions others like him in his first epistle when he says, "They went out from us, but *they were not of us*; for if they had been of us, they would have continued with us. But they went out, that it might become plain that they all are not of us. But you have been anointed by the Holy One [indwelt by his Spirit]" (1 John 2:19–20, emphasis added).

In the second category, we are given several examples of Christian men and women whom Satan successfully tripped up, causing them to turn from following the Lord, no longer being fruit bearers for the Lord. Paul is not surprised by this because if Satan is unsuccessful in preventing from coming *to Christ*, his next goal is to make them ineffective *for Christ*. The Christian life in this world isn't easy. Paul uses such words as "strayed after" (1 Timothy 5:15), "in the snare of the devil" (1 Timothy 6:9), and "being captured by him" (2 Timothy 2:26), all relating to believers. Satan without a doubt is the god of this world, and we are in essence living behind enemy lines in his territory during our lives down here. One such example of a person who had strayed is the adulterer Paul wrote about in both 1 and 2 Corinthians. "You are to deliver this man to Satan for the destruction of the flesh, so that his spirit may be saved in the day of the Lord" (1 Corinthians 4:20).

So we see his sin didn't negate his salvation but rather led to his need for discipline with the purpose of restoration, and it seems to have been effective. We see what is likely the same man spoken of once again in Paul's second letter. "For such a one, this punishment by the majority is enough, so you should rather turn to forgive and comfort him, or he may be overwhelmed by excessive sorrow. So I beg you to reaffirm your love for him" (2 Corinthians 2:6–8).

On this same topic, Paul tells Timothy what a good shepherd is to do for those who are straying. He tells us he is to "correct his opponents with gentleness. God may perhaps grant them repentance leading to a knowledge of the truth, and they may escape from *the snare of the devil*, after being captured by him to do his will" (2 Timothy 2:25–26, emphasis added).

Even wrong doctrine doesn't negate a salvation we already possess, but the road can become very hard for the believer who seeks to go his own way. Paul tells Timothy to "wage the good warfare, holding faith and a good conscience. By rejecting this, some have made shipwreck of their faith, among whom are Hymenaeus and Alexander, whom I have handed over to Satan that they may learn not to blaspheme" (1 Timothy 1:18–20).

So even with those turning away from the faith and a good conscience, Paul had confidence that they would return. God would still continue to work in their hearts through allowing them to go through perhaps painful learning experiences, God's discipline, through Satan's actions in their lives.

Then again we have this assurance given in 1 Corinthians 1:9. "God is faithful, by whom you were called into the fellowship of his Son, Jesus Christ our Lord." Thankfully, our preservation as God's children is certain and his job even when we are not. Paul told the believers in Ephesus, "He chose us in him before the foundation of the world, that we should be holy and blameless before him. In love he predestined us for adoption through Jesus Christ, according to the purpose of his will, to the praise of his glorious grace, with which he has blessed us in the Beloved" (Ephesians 1:4–6).

So God promises those who have trusted in his Son as Savior that he will ensure they will end up in heaven and will be with him in perfect holiness and blamelessness as his true sons and daughters. At times our faith is weak, but praise God our preservation is his concern, and it is certain.

Also, as his children, part of the family, we are now called to use the spiritual gifts given to us by the Holy Spirit during this life for the benefit of the church, our brothers and sisters in the Lord. See these verses first. "Having gifts that differ according to the grace given to us, let us use them: if prophecy, in proportion to our faith; if service, in our serving; the one who teaches, in his teaching; the one who exhorts, in his exhortation; the one who contributes, in generosity; the one who leads, with zeal; the one who does acts of mercy, with cheerfulness" (Romans 12:6–8).

Also, Paul says,

> Now concerning spiritual gifts … there are varieties of gifts, but the same Spirit … To each is given the manifestation of the Spirit for the common good. (1 Corinthians 12:1, 4, 7)

> Rather speaking the truth in love, we are to grow up in every way into him who is the head, into Christ, from whom the whole body, joined and held together by every joint with which it is equipped, when each part is working properly, makes the body grow so that it builds itself up in love. (Ephesians 4:15–16)

So to be part of the family God, to be in Christ, isn't just a positional truth but a place of security from which each of us can be useful, functioning as the Lord's ambassadors and workers together for the benefit of the whole body of Christ. It's certainly possible to do this poorly and have much of our work for the Lord following our salvation be lost, as Paul tells us in 1 Corinthians. "If anyone's work is burned up, he will suffer loss, though he himself will be saved, but only as through fire" (3:15).

Chapter Five

Ordo Salutis

When it comes to salvation, many Christian religious branches and denominations have proposed vastly different lists and sequences as to *the steps of salvation* as well as the order in which they occur. A frequent change, for instance, is to put regeneration before faith, which is done in a supposed attempt to protect God's sovereignty, but in effect, it actually negates the free will given to us by God. Some traditions even adds steps such as election. We do acknowledge that some of these events occur simultaneously, but it is important to look again at Scripture to see what appears to be God's plan as to the steps of salvation and the order in which they take place.

❖ SALVATION PROVIDED

First and of most importance is for us realize that this was God's project, planned from a past eternity because of his love to provide salvation to fallen humanity. This plan is first inferred in the Garden of Eden after man's disobedience. There Lord speaks to Satan, who was shapeshifting as the serpent, concerning his coming judgment to be through "the offspring of the woman," referring to the Lord Jesus. "I will put enmity between you and the woman, and between your offspring and her offspring; he shall bruise your head, and you shall bruise his [masculine, singular noun] heel" (Genesis 3:15). Then later we read in the New Testament, "Since therefore the children share in flesh and blood, he himself likewise partook of the same things, that through death he might destroy the one who has the power of death, that is, the devil and deliver all those who through fear of death were subject to lifelong slavery" (Hebrews 2:14–15).

The coming of God the Son, incarnate into this world as a man, was about more than just defeating Satan. The purpose was to give himself as a willing sacrifice for our sins, without which there could be no salvation. He did this at Calvary, fully paying the price for our disobedience and rebellion against God. "If, because of one man's trespass, death reigned through that one man, much more will those who receive the abundance of grace and the free gift of righteousness reign in life through the one man, Jesus Christ" (Romans 5:17).

Now let's look at the steps that take this finished work at Calvary to a finished work in us

1. **The Calling of the Holy Spirit**: With salvation planned and provided, there is the Holy Spirit's personal calling of people out of the darkness of sin and Satan's domain, drawing them back to God. Choosing to respond, people are given further illumination of their condition and need, but alternatively choosing instead to reject will result in the further hardening of their hearts. Jesus said, "And I, when I am lifted up from the earth, will draw all people to myself" (John 12:32). Then later we read,

   > Nevertheless, I tell you the truth: it is to your advantage that I go away, for if I do not go away, the Helper will not come to you. But if I go, I will send him to you. And when he comes, he will convict the world concerning sin and righteousness and judgment. (John 16:7–8)

   > For God, who said, "Let light shine out of darkness," has shone in our hearts to give the light of the knowledge

of the glory of God in the face of Jesus Christ. (2 Corinthians 4:6)

2. **Conviction**: This occurs in people's hearts in response to the accusation of their consciences and the Spirit's call, causing a recognition of their sin and guilt before God. The primary tool here is the sword of the Spirit, meaning holy Scripture. Responding to this need for God's salvation, as revealed by the Spirit, will take us to the next step, but we can reject it as well and shut it out or turn from it and harden ourselves to the truth. Paul, reminiscing while on his missionary journey, said, "Our gospel came to you not only in word, but also in power and in the Holy Spirit and with full conviction" (1 Thessalonians 1:5).

3. **Repentance**: Each person is called to respond by *repenting* from his or her sin, rebellion, and living for self as an act of free will. This is a result of personal conviction of sin and is a deliberate turning from self and Satan's ways to God and turning to his Son as the only way of salvation. Repentance is an act of acknowledgment of the sinner's need and his or her helplessness before a holy God. This "internal resolve to turn from one's sins," as David R. Anderson wrote,[10] most often opens the will to taking that next step. Luke tells us the following:

    > Thus it is written, that the Christ should suffer and on the third day rise from the dead, and that repentance and forgiveness of sins should be proclaimed in his name to all nations, beginning from Jerusalem. (Luke 24:46–48)

    > Now when they heard this they were cut to the heart [convicted of sin], and said to Peter and the rest of the apostles, "Brothers, what shall we do?" And Peter said to them, "Repent and be baptized every one of you in the name of Jesus Christ for the forgiveness of your sins, and you will receive the gift of the Holy Spirit." (Acts 2:37–38)

4. **Faith**: Once we have turned from our own way, there then must be that necessary personal acceptance of the Lord Jesus Christ as our Savior, a decision to follow him. Salvation is, Paul says in Romans 3, to be received "as a gift" (see also Romans 3:23–26). John says, "He came to his own, and his own people did not receive him. But to all who did receive him, who believed in his name, he gave the right to become children of God" (John 1:11–12). Then Paul tells us we access this salvation through faith.

"Therefore, since we have been justified by faith, we have peace with God through our Lord Jesus Christ. Through him we have also obtained access by faith into this grace in which we stand, and we rejoice in hope of the glory of God" (Romans 5:1–2).

Immediately following this step of faith, several important things occur simultaneously as follows (steps 6–9), but the final two (steps 10–11), being made fully holy in our walk and being glorified, still await us.

5. **Justification and Forgiveness**: To be justified is God's judicious act of declaring a person no longer condemned because of sin but made righteous before him on the basis of Christ's sufficient and efficacious sacrifice at Calvary. It is this finished work at Calvary where the new believer in his or her new faith is now resting. The other part of this is forgiveness now able to be imparted by a holy God. This is God's declaration of that person's sins no longer standing between his holiness and the sinner, who has now been made right before him because of Calvary.

> Let it be known to you therefore, brothers, that through this man forgiveness of sins is proclaimed to you, and by him everyone who believes is freed from everything from which you could not be freed by the law of Moses. (Acts 13:38–39)

> For I will be merciful toward their iniquities, and *I will remember their sins no more*. (Hebrews 8:12, emphasis added)

6. **Regeneration and the Indwelling of the Holy Spirit**: This is what God does for each person who comes to him by faith. He gives us new spiritual life in Christ when we are born again of the Spirit, reconciled back to God, and brought into a new and living relationship with him. In this new relationship, we are called to walk before him in love and live as ambassadors for him in this world. We are enabled to do so by the power of his Spirit within us. Paul wrote, "He saved us, not because of works done by us in righteousness, but according to his own mercy, by the washing of regeneration and renewal of the Holy Spirit" (Titus 3:5). Further, he wrote, "You, however, are not in the flesh but in the Spirit, if in fact the Spirit of God dwells in you. Anyone who does not have the Spirit of Christ does not belong to him" (Romans 8:9).

7. **Illumination**: This partly begins prior to salvation (see step 2) as a person becomes receptive to God's working on his or her heart and is drawn to the Savior, yet it is particularly present following salvation because of the indwelling presence of the Holy Spirit, who, John 16:13 says, "will guide you into all truth." Through the Holy Spirit, we can then experience his ongoing guidance in our lives, especially through the Scriptures. "I write these things to you about those who are trying to deceive you. But the anointing that you received from him abides in you, and you have no need that anyone should teach you. But as his anointing teaches you about everything—and is true and is no lie, just as it has taught you—abide in him" (1 John 2:26–27).

8. **Eternal Security**. This part comes through adoption as sons. As sinners saved by grace through the death of his Son and having been given new spiritual life, God brings us into a living relationship with him as part of his family. And with his plans already made for our future including usefulness in this life and his coming kingdom, he then gives us the Holy Spirit. Not only is the Spirit's presence in us the seal of our being sons, but he is also the sanctifier in our lives. In addition, he is the guarantor of our future inheritance. In addition, the resurrected Christ, who lives eternally, will advocate

for us before the Father. We are utterly secure in him. See John 10:27–29 as well as this guarantee in Ephesians 1.

> "In him you also, when you heard the word of truth, the gospel of your salvation, and believed in him, were sealed with the promised Holy Spirit, who is the guarantee of our inheritance until we acquire possession of it, to the praise of his glory" (vv. 13–14).

9. **Sanctification**: God sees us believers as already "in Christ" and as a part of his body; therefore, we are positionally holy following our salvation. In practice, however, this is a lifelong and at times painful process of the Holy Spirit working within us to make us more like Christ. He has given this guarantee to all believers who are, even now, seen as being "in Christ" from a past eternity (Roman 6:19; Ephesians 1:3–4; 1 Peter 1:15). As we increase in Christlikeness, our fellowship with him, along with our fruitfulness for him, also increases (John 15:1–11). "For by a single offering he has perfected for all time those who are *being sanctified*" (Hebrew 10:14, emphasis added). The evidence of it is in our lives. "But the fruit of the Spirit is love, joy, peace, patience, kindness, goodness, faithfulness, gentleness, self-control; against such things there is no law" (Galatians 5:22–24).

10. **Glorification**: With the sin nature fully removed, we will all be at his coming resurrected and with glorified, spiritual bodies made imperishable and immortal. We will be fit to reign with Christ eternally. What a hope we have before us! (See also Romans 8:16–17.) "Just as we have borne the image of the man of dust, we shall also bear the image of the man of heaven." And "Behold! I tell you a mystery. We shall not all sleep, but we shall all be changed, in a moment, in the twinkling of an eye, at the last trumpet. For the trumpet will sound, and the dead will be raised imperishable, and we shall be changed" (1 Corinthians 15:49, 51–53).

Chapter Six

Answering the Questions

Finally, if there is still some concern or confusion as to what the Bible says about any of these issues, let's briefly try to answer the questions asked back at the end of the introduction and that have troubled so many (though there will be some redundancy here). I do this with some hesitancy, realizing my own limitations, biases, and views; but I trust Scripture will keep us on the right path. Some may have a conflict with my current understanding of these issues, but I would urge you to take the time to look up the passages referenced and see them for yourself in their actual context in Scripture to assure yourself, as far as possible, of their meaning. Then think each issue through, asking for the Lord's help and discernment.

* WAS CHRIST'S DEATH AT CALVARY SUFFICIENT TO
  PAY THE PRICE FOR THE SALVATION OF EVERY HUMAN
  BEING FOR ALL THEIR SINS AND FOR ALL TIME?

The answer must first be founded on the love of God, a core character of his person, which isn't constrained but goes out to all the world, to all he has uniquely made in his image. See the confirmation from Scripture.

All we like sheep have gone astray; we have turned everyone to his own way; and the Lord has laid on him the iniquity *of us all*. (Isaiah 53:6, emphasis added)

And the angel said to them, "Fear not, for behold, I bring you good news of a great joy that will be *for all the people*." (Luke 2:10, emphasis added)

For God so loved *the world*, that he gave his only Son, that *whoever* believes in him should not perish but have eternal life. (John 3:16, emphasis added)

Therefore, as one trespass [of Adam] led to condemnation for all men, so one act of righteousness [of Christ Jesus] leads to justification and life *for all men*. (Romans 5:18, emphasis added)

For the grace of God has appeared, bringing salvation *for all people*. (Titus 2:11, emphasis added)

Since therefore the children share in flesh and blood, he himself likewise partook of the same things, that through death he might destroy the one who has the power of death, that is, the devil, and *deliver all* those who through fear of death were subject to lifelong slavery. (Hebrews 2:14–15, emphasis added)

He is the propitiation for our sins, and not for ours only but also *for the sins of the whole world*. (1 John 2:2, emphasis added)

This extensive list is certainly not exhaustive but clearly shows us the common thread through all these verses of God's great love for all mankind. And we must be careful not to give special meanings to the *italicised* phrases to limit them but to take them in their normal sense and usage. They give us great assurance concerning the extent of this salvation, which is offered, as is made so abundantly clear, to "all people."

Second, in addition to being based on the character of God, love is also contingent on the worth of the one making the sacrifice. In this case, it was the eternal Son of God, who came into the world as Jesus, the sinless Son of Man, while yet continuing to retain his deity. Therefore, his sacrifice was of infinite worth. Think of that—of infinite worth! People have struggled with the question of whose sin Christ paid for. They have agonized over whether he paid the price for their sins. But in Hebrews we are told why his sacrifice was different. "Consequently, he is able to save to *the uttermost* those who draw near to God through him, since he always lives to make intercession for them. For it was indeed fitting that we should have such a high priest, holy, innocent, unstained, separated from sinners, and exalted above the heavens. He has no need, like those high priests, to offer sacrifices daily, first for his own sins and then for those of the people, since he did this once for all when he offered up himself" (Hebrews 7:25–28, emphasis added).

Satan has had a field day in the minds of many sincere believers, who anxiously wonder whether they are among the elect (meaning those of a limited number chosen for salvation), those for whom Christ suffered and therefore truly saved. They've believed the lie that if they weren't saved and were still dead in their sins, they wouldn't even know it. However, it's important for you to know that you won't find that pernicious doctrine of limited atonement in the Scriptures. Instead, God's choosing was for those he foreknew would accept his salvation, and the choosing was for those who would be given particular roles and work in his kingdom as he has preordained for them.

So these verses seen above from Hebrews 7 confirm for us that the sufficiency of our salvation is found in the character and person of Christ, who offered himself willingly as the perfect, holy sacrifice. Now in the power of an endless life, he is also the guarantor of it.

Do you believe Jesus is God's Son and came into the world to save sinners through his death on the cross? Has there been a time when you were convicted of your sins and turned to the Lord for salvation? And did you accept him as your Savior? If so, then what does Scripture say? "*To all who did receive him*, who believed in his name, *he gave the right to become children of God*" (John 1:12, emphasis added).

This is an important verse. You need to look it up in your Bible and make it your verse. Underline it! Reread it regularly. Satan has no right to steal your joy and peace when what God wants for you is to live daily in the joy of your salvation and in the certainty of his promises. It would be a sin not to believe this promise from God.

William MacDonald in his *Believer's Bible Commentary* comments on the importance of the last phrase in John 3:16: "whoever believes in Him should not perish."[11] So while there is no need for anyone to perish, yet the possibility remains. This takes us to the next question below.

✦ WILL ALL PEOPLE BE EVENTUALLY SAVED?

Scripture tells us that God has made a provision for all people to come to him for salvation. Also, the Holy Spirit is in the world, as we read in John 16, "convict[ing] the world [that's all people in the world] concerning sin and righteousness and judgment." And he encourages them to come, even urges them through the convicting power of his Spirit to come, but the choice remains theirs. See what John also said in the first chapter of his Gospel, showing there were exclusions, not as to who could be saved but as to who would be saved through turning or failing to turn in faith to the Savior. "He came to his own, and *his own people did not receive him*. But *to all who did receive him, who believed in his name*, he gave the right to become children of God, *who were born*, not of blood nor of the will of the flesh nor of the will of man, but *of God*" (John 1: 11–13, emphasis added).

The miracle of the new birth was and continues to be wholly a work of God, but the choice of receiving it was theirs. So people were making their choices back then as well as now. Some received Christ as Savior, while others rebelled against him. People may recoil at the idea of God sending anyone to hell—and rightly so, for it is a terrible, unending punishment. Yet see what Jesus told his disciples concerning the judgment of the nation at the end of the tribulation. "Then he will say to those on his left, 'Depart from me, you cursed, into the *eternal fire prepared for the devil and his angels*. For I was hungry, and you gave me no food, I was thirsty, and you gave me no drink, I was a stranger, and you did not welcome me, naked and you did not clothe me, sick and in prison and you did not visit me'" (Matthew 25:41–43, emphasis added).

Human choice was the deciding factor for this judgment of God. We know that because for the angels who rebelled, with eyes wide open, there would be no reprieve, no second chance; God's holiness must be served. But the inference in the Lord's statement here is that for people, those made in his image and on whom he set his love, it was different. Although lost because of their sin, still they were offered salvation. But then in choosing to reject God's ways and the Lord who had provided it for them, they were condemning themselves to a lost eternity. That is the thing about human beings truly having free will—it carries with it great responsibility and profound consequences. Look back again at what Jesus once said about Jerusalem. You can hear the sadness in his voice when he ends by saying, "And *you would not!*" (Matthew 23:37, emphasis added).

The heretical view of universalism propounded in the modern era by the theology of the neo-Calvinist Karl Barth was rejuvenated by Rob Bell in his book *Love Wins.* Essentially, Bell said that God's love wins out over God's holiness. In Reformed theology, the situation is the reverse; God's holiness wins out over God's love. Yet careful biblical exegesis shows Bell's view has no scriptural basis and goes against the totality of God's character, which includes both his love and holiness at all times.

I remember many years ago when I was completing a master's degree in bioethics. I was debating which ethics guideline should take precedence over another. For example, "lying" or "saving a life" by lying, and the professor tried to get us sucked into "situation ethics," which in the end leave us without any foundation.

Bell redefines hell as simply wrong thinking on our part. Read his words on page 140 of his book. "Hell is our refusal to trust God's retelling of our story." He says then that hell isn't an actual place. In addition, he believes that however a person may live, what Christ accomplished at Calvary has cleansed the sins of all people, so all of us are now his children. But read these two longer passages from Bell's *Love Wins* to get a better picture of what he's saying. First, consider his opening page.

"Of all the billions of people who have ever lived, will only a select number 'make it to a better place' and every single other person suffer in torment and punishment forever? Is this acceptable to God? ... What kind of God is that?" (pp. 1–2). Bell is really arguing his case by comparing two wrong theologies—Calvinism versus universalism. Where is the Bible in this? Read further in his book.

> We believe all sorts of things about ourselves. What the gospel does is confront our version of our story with God's version of our story. It is a brutally honest, exuberantly liberating story, and it is good news.
>
> It begins with the sure and certain truth that we are loved. That in spite of whatever has gone horribly wrong deep in our hearts and has spread to every corner of the world, in spite of our sins, failures, rebellion, and hard hearts, in spite of what's been done to us or what we've done, *God has made peace with us.*
>
> Done. Complete. As Jesus said, "It is finished."
>
> We are now invited to live a whole new life without guilt or shame or blame or anxiety. We are going to be fine. (pp. 140–141)[12]

Sadly, here we see no need for conviction or repentance or by faith receiving Christ as Savior. Bell says in essence that hell is merely wrong thinking on our part. What a terrible lie of Satan! And certainly, God's holiness is nowhere to be seen. The implication suggested in the title of his book is that in the end God's love trumps his holiness, which because of the immutability of his character cannot be. All his attributes are always active at all times and can never contradict one another in all he does or says. Rob Bell, in wanting to correct wrong teaching from the past, especially legalism and Calvinism, has in essence come up with a new religion, with salvation based on the psychology of getting your thinking right. But what does Scripture say?

In a future eternity, Scripture informs us there really are only two places for a person to be. We will either be in a real place with the Lord by turning from our sin and accepting him as Savior, in which case he is able to make us holy and fit for heaven, or turn from his love and reject him, ending up in a lost eternity, a very real place indeed. Since God in his love provided a great salvation for us, the critical choice of our eternal destiny then becomes ours alone. Tragically, *by their own choice*, many will not accept salvation and will enter into eternity still under God's condemnation, as we're told in John 3:18, 36. With death, their choice becomes unalterable, for their names weren't written in the Lamb's Book of Life during this life. See the passages below that confirm this eternal judgment.

> Then he will answer them, saying, "Truly, I say to you, as you did not do it to one of the least of these, you did not do it to me." And these will go away into *eternal punishment*, but the righteous into eternal life." (Matthew 25:45–46, emphasis added)

> Those who do not know God and on those who do not obey the gospel of our Lord Jesus. They will suffer the punishment of *eternal destruction*, away from the presence of the Lord and from the glory of his might. (2 Thessalonians 1:8–9, emphasis added)

> And finally, Woe to them! For they walked in the way of Cain and abandoned themselves for the sake of gain to Balaam's error and perished in Korah's rebellion. These are blemishes on your love feasts, as they feast with you without fear, looking after themselves; waterless clouds, swept along by winds; fruitless trees in late autumn, twice dead, uprooted; wild waves of the sea, casting up the foam of their own shame; wandering stars, for whom *the gloom of utter darkness has been reserved forever.* (Jude 11–13, emphasis added)

We cannot but feel horror at the finality of this unalterable end for any person. But a God of love will still be holy. While we may push back against this, we do so still having within us an imperfect understanding because of our sin nature. In the future, made perfect in Christ, we will understand and bow in worship at both the holiness and goodness of God.

Also, alternatively, what we must not believe is that with our death, like animals, we will simply cease to be. We are, as made in God's image, both mortal and spiritual beings, and we will exist forever. Many Scriptures confirm this. See the story Jesus told in Luke 16 of two men who lived vastly different lives here on earth but then died. Jesus tells us, "The poor man died and was carried by the angels to Abraham's side. The rich man also died and was buried, and in Hades, being in torment, he lifted up his eyes and saw Abraham far off and Lazarus at his side" (Luke 16:22–24).

Luke, the writer, doesn't indicate that this is a parable. And the fact that the Lord starts this story by saying, "There was a man" and then later names the other man as Lazarus removes this from the realm of being a generic parable to being about real people and real events, making it a very sobering lesson indeed.

❖ WHAT ABOUT THOSE WHO HAVE NEVER HEARD THE GOSPEL? WILL THEY ALL PERISH?

Let's establish some "knowns" when discussing this difficult question. First, let's determine the condition of mankind from the Scriptures. "And the Lord God commanded the man, saying, 'You may surely eat of every tree of the garden, but of the tree of the knowledge of good and evil you shall not eat, for in the day that you eat of it you shall surely die'" (Genesis 2:16–17).

So the fact is: As human beings, we have been created with free will to obey is disobey our Creator.

> "For the wrath of God is revealed from heaven against all ungodliness and unrighteousness of men, who by their unrighteousness suppress the truth. For what can be known about God is plain to them, because God has shown it to them. For his invisible attributes, namely, his eternal power and divine nature, have been clearly perceived, ever since the creation of the world, in the

things that have been made. So they are without excuse"
(Romans 1:18–21).

So the fact is: We are all innately aware that there is a God and that
he is our almighty Creator.

"For when Gentiles, who do not have the law, by nature
do what the law requires, they are a law to themselves,
even though they do not have the law. They show that
the work of the law is written on their hearts, while their
conscience also bears witness, and their conflicting
thoughts accuse or even excuse them on that day when,
according to my gospel, God judges the secrets of men
by Christ Jesus" (Romans 2:14–16).

So the fact is: We each have been endowed with a moral conscience
to know right and wrong.

"Now we know that whatever the law says it speaks to
those who are under the law, so that every mouth may be
stopped, and the whole world may be held accountable
to God. For by works of the law no human being will
be justified in his sight, since through the law comes
knowledge of sin" (Romans 3:19–20).

So the fact is: We know we are imperfect and fall short of God's glory
and therefore are sinners.

"And if anyone's name was not found written in the book
of life, he was thrown into the lake of fire" (Revelation
20:15).

So the fact is: As humans, we know we need to be made right with
God to escape coming judgment. Why do you think man has invented
so many religious systems if not to find a way back to God? A man's
name isn't written in the Book of Life because of a person choosing to
turn away from God's Spirit's calling.

So God has revealed himself to us as human beings in his world, and yet our response too often is to suppress this truth. Our condemnation before a holy God then is clear and certain, and our judgment will be just. What then is God's position as we stand before him with our guilt? Amazingly, he loves us still; as John wrote in John 3:16, "For God so loved the *world*" (emphasis added). He is speaking here of the whole of humanity. And God's love moved him to act by sending his Son as the sacrifice for sin. But in addition, he has now sent his Spirit into the world to draw people to himself. See what Jesus said in these two passages in John's Gospel.

> "And I, when I am lifted up from the earth, will draw *all people* to myself." (John 12:32, emphasis added)

> "If I do not go away, the Helper will not come to you. But if I go, I will send him to you. And when he comes, he will convict *the world* concerning sin and righteousness and judgment: concerning sin, because they do not believe in me." (John 16:7–9, emphasis added)

The Holy Spirit continues his work in this world, even today, of drawing all people to himself. Oh, that more would respond and move toward the light of the truth being revealed to them!

In particular, the Spirit uses the Word of God to bring people to repentance and salvation; yet even within ourselves and within our world, there is sufficient evidence for us to realize our need before our God and seek him. Paul speaks about this need, referencing the Old Testament. "Then Isaiah [65:1] is so bold as to say, 'I have been found by those who did not seek me; *I have shown myself* to those who did not ask for me'" (Romans 10:20, emphasis added).

Know this—that all those who seek the Lord in sincerity will be found by him. Yes, only through Christ can we be saved, but the gospel will reach the sincere seeker. This reminds me of the Ethiopian eunuch, who truly was a seeker for the true God without having heard about Jesus. God ensured that Philip, the evangelist, found him, shared with him the good news, and guided him into the kingdom. I believe the Bible tells us that no one who is a seeker of God will end up in hell. Listen to what the writer of Hebrews says in chapter 11. "Whoever would draw near to God must believe that he exists and that he rewards *those who seek him*" (Hebrews 11:1, 5, emphasis added).

A similar miraculous phenomenon is being seen today among many Muslims, who are sincerely seeking God. Often the story is told of them having a dream and then seeing a person they instinctively know to be Jesus calling to them. They wake and immediately start an urgent search for a Bible or a Christian who can tell them about Christ.

This also reminds me of the story Don Richardson tells in his book *Peace Child* (1974)[13] about the vengeful Sawi people of Irian Jaya, who were caught up in their endless revenge slayings, but then also their way of making peace with their enemies. When even they became weary of the killings, a man from each of the two warring tribes took one of his own young children and handed the child over to the other tribe. As long as the child lived, peace held. I certainly agree with this missionary, who was convinced that this was God's way of preparing them to receive and understand the gospel. God gave his own Son, who ever lives, for their salvation.

Also, another relevant story from Scripture is found in Genesis 18, where we see the Lord coming down to bring judgment on sinful Sodom, and we read of Abraham pleading for mercy for Lot and his family. He was asking for the loving-kindness of God when he said, "Shall not the Judge of all the earth do what is just?" (Genesis 18:25).

We might ask then, "What would it mean for God to act justly in this case?" I believe Abraham was challenging the Lord to act according to the totality of his immutable nature. Abraham had every right to plead for this, for he knew that though God was holy and so must act on his holiness at all times, yet even in his righteous anger, he must never act at the same time to negate the core character of his love.

Over the years, people often have viewed God either as the righteous, holy judge or alternatively as the gracious lover of our souls and forgiver of sins. As we soak our hearts in Scripture and seek to understand the intrinsic glory of his person, we must come to see the whole as so much more than his individual attributes, wonderful as they are. Don't make God too small in your thinking.

❖ Can or Must We Contribute to Our Salvation? Here Is the Issue of Good Works.

Despite the clarity of God's Word, men have consistently tried to include human efforts or works in their salvation. But read what the Scriptures say in these passages.

> For *by works of the law no human being will be justified in his sight,* since through the law comes knowledge of sin. (Romans 3:20, emphasis added)

> And to the one *who does not work* but trusts him who justifies the ungodly, his faith is counted as righteousness. (Romans 4:5, emphasis added)

> We also have believed in Christ Jesus, in order to be justified by faith in Christ and *not by works* of the law, because *by works of the law no one will be justified.* (Galatians 2:16, emphasis added)

> For by grace you have been saved through faith. And this is not your own doing; it is the gift of God, *not a result of works, so that no one may boast.* (Ephesians 2:8–9, emphasis added)

Scripture has said over and over that we cannot contribute our so-called good works toward our salvation. Yet this recovered truth, called "*sola gratia*" (grace alone), caused a seismic shift in church doctrine in the mid-1500s. At the Council of Trent, the Roman Catholic Church pushed back against this biblical teaching by saying,[5] "Quote: 'If anyone saith that justifying faith is nothing else but confidence in the divine mercy which remits sin for Christ's sake alone; or, that this confidence alone is that whereby we are justified, let him be anathema.' Session VI, Canon 12."[14]

So where do works fit in? It is certainly evident from these verses quoted above that trusting in Jesus isn't a work in itself. However, work is connected to faith in several passages of Scripture, such as Ephesians

2, where it comes in its right place, following faith and as a confirmation of it. "For we are his workmanship, created in Christ Jesus *for good works*, which God prepared beforehand, that we should walk in them" (Ephesians 2:10, emphasis added).

Also, James speaks to their necessity. "So also faith by itself, if it does not have works, is dead" (James 2:17). This means we can now change the way we live if we've been redeemed and indwelt with God's Spirit. Our very desires will change; we also see this truth in 2 Corinthians 8, where Paul assumes that as Christians these people will exhibit good works. "And in this matter, I give my judgment: this benefits you, who a year ago started not only to do this work but also to desire to do it" (2 Corinthians 8:10–11).

Clearly, both Paul and James make the same point that it is impossible to have faith, to be truly saved, but there be no evidence of it in our lives. As believers, we will inevitably show this faith by a change in our lives, by works. A person who puts his or her faith in the finished work of Christ will be made spiritually alive. Through this new life, we are then and only then through the desire of the new nature and the power of the indwelling Spirit able to do the works of God. Paul speaks to the necessity of this new life. "If the Spirit of him who raised Jesus from the dead dwells in you, he who raised Christ Jesus from the dead will also give life to your mortal bodies through his Spirit who dwells in you" (Romans 8:11).

It is then through the power of the Holy Spirit and this new life that we can do the works of God. This is the meaning of 1 Thessalonians 1:3, where Paul talks about the Christian's "work of faith," a true sign of his or her salvation, and that necessarily occurs as a result of his or her faith.

Could it possibly be any plainer? Yet despite this, people have been ingenious at finding ways to include the necessity of works in their salvation. We see this in other religions as well. The balancing of the scale of good deeds and bad is at the core of Islam for gaining paradise. In Christendom from about AD 400 and on into the Middle Ages, many admired monasticism as a way to truly earn God's favor and therefore their eternal salvation. Others went on pilgrimages to Jerusalem or other holy sites. Still others even today are taught that Christ's sacrifice at Calvary opens the door to salvation for us, but then it is up to us and how we live our lives to be justified before him.

But know that this isn't biblical truth. First, know that we don't have to earn our Lord's love; he already loves us. He provided salvation for us because of his love. Second, his work at Calvary truly satisfied the Father in respect to all our sins. Third, it's not up to us to remain one of God's children. See the promises given in John 10 and Ephesians 1. Yes, as Christians, we are given responsibilities to live for God during this life, but holding on to our salvation isn't one of them. He will keep us safe in his hand.

To help those professing to be Christians but not walking in faith, the Catholic Church made a new doctrine just for them; this was also of benefit to the coffers of the church. It was called "purgatory." Purgatory, we are told, is a way of suffering for a period to finish paying God for the debt of our sins before being allowed into heaven. Other people still living and concerned about their sins could contribute their prayers or money to the church to shorten their time. This completely fabricated doctrine is another form of salvation through works. This is just one example of many ways that have been invented over the years to attempt to get ourselves in on this work of redemption. But the truth is that we could never pay any of this debt if we tried. Our best efforts would always be tainted by our sins. Tragically if a person dies while still in that state of condemnation under God, that person will be forever lost. Salvation is all of God, available during our lives here on earth and received solely by faith.

❖ Can All Come and Be Saved? Has God Made Salvation Available for Everyone?

This is similar to the first question about the sufficiency of God's salvation. Here it is about the *availability* of it. We must remember that God does nothing that doesn't agree in all aspects with his unchanging character. There is no mystery involved here as some would propose. He is love and so has not only created mankind but set his love on us. He does not play favorites, and he will never go back on his promises or show partiality or favoritism. See what the apostle Paul says in Romans 2. "There will be tribulation and distress for every human being who does evil, the Jew first and also the Greek, but glory and honor and peace for everyone who does good, the Jew first and also the Greek. For *God shows no partiality*" (vv. 9–11, emphasis added).

Doing evil means acting contrary to God's will and character and remaining in rebellion against him. Therefore, because he shows "no partiality," we are all, as John 3:18 tells us, "condemned." We all need his salvation. How wonderful then it is in that same chapter to read the words of the preceding verses.

> For God so loved the world, that he gave his only Son, that *whoever* believes in him should not perish but have eternal life. For God did not send his Son into the world to condemn the world, but in order *that the world might be saved* through him. (John 3:16–17, emphasis added)

> Jesus also commanded us, "Go into *all the world* and proclaim the gospel to_*the whole creation. Whoever believes and is baptized will be saved*, but whoever does not believe will be condemned." (Mark 16:15–16, emphasis added)

> The Lord is not slow to fulfill his promise as some count slowness, but is patient toward you, *not wishing that any should perish*, but that all should reach repentance. (2 Peter 3:9, emphasis added)

This doesn't imply, however, that all will be saved since people have been given free will and the ability to choose to accept or reject this great salvation provided for them.

Some theologians look doubtfully at the concept of human free will, feeling that this somehow diminishes the sovereignty of God since God is subjecting himself to the will of another. But this creation of people in his own image is an amazing thing God has done with the plan of lifting the people he has created into a place of fellowship with the Creator himself. Amazingly, in his sovereignty he allows people to actually reject what he desires for them.

Others, in attempting to justify God's offering a limited salvation only for those he chose in a past eternity, emphasize the glory of his holiness above all his other attributes including his love. Read what Matt Papa has to say from his Calvinist perspective. "God's holiness is not so much an attribute of God as it is the foundation of all his attributes."[15]

So he attempts to set this one attribute above all others, and that would of course include love. This would seem to be justification for God to do as he wishes even regarding salvation. But he cannot just do anything! God must and desires to act at all times in accord with his eternal attributes and eternal and unchanging character.

The Jewish leadership chose to reject the Lord's offer many times, causing Jesus to lament, as we saw previously in Matthew 23:37–38, but while desiring them to come and accept his offer of forgiveness, he wouldn't force them.

Of course, our God, being omniscient, knows the end from the beginning and therefore knows who will accept or reject his offer of salvation. But there is nothing in Scripture to indicate that the fact of his knowing was predicated on a judicial act of his foreordaining their choice. To say he couldn't know unless it had first been his decision would be to diminish his deity and omniscience! Being outside of time, he simply knows and yet amazingly still calls all to repent and be saved.

❖ Does God Need to Regenerate a Person or Give Spiritual Life before He or She Can Then Necessarily Believe?

Regeneration is all a work of God but is enacted only for those who in faith come to him for salvation. Paul was speaking about Abraham and his faith in Romans 4 but then applied this when he wrote, "Therefore, since we have been justified by faith, we have peace with God through our Lord Jesus Christ. Through him we have also obtained access by faith into this grace in which we stand, and we rejoice in hope of the glory of God" (Romans 5:1–2).

Romans 3–5 emphasize people's personal faith as necessary for their salvation. The passage never, in fact, talks about God giving a person faith to believe. To say that an unbelieving person doesn't have free will is to take away his or her responsibility for his or her choices and actions. Abraham, referred to above, was also credited as having righteousness because of his faith.

We see, in fact, that God does hold each of us responsible. Also, regarding salvation, for a person to believe doesn't mean just mean thinking something is true. Satan also believes (James 2:19); instead, it carries with it the wider idea of trusting or receiving and of making a personal choice of assent based on that belief. It is certainly true that Satan attempts to blind us to God's truth and that we are also rebellious by natural inclination, wanting to go our own way. That is why Scripture tells us that the Holy Spirit counteracts Satan's activity and works in our hearts to illuminate us to God's truth and draw (not drag) us to God. The wonderful provision is from God, but the responsibility and choice remain firmly with us.

Indeed, people weakened by sin and blinded by Satan wouldn't choose to believe in the Lord Jesus as Savior without the intervention of the Holy Spirit and his working in their hearts. "No one can come to me unless the Father, who sent me, draws him" (John 6:44). But he does do this, enabled to work in people's hearts because we have been made moral beings. More than that, we again read, "He [the Holy Spirit] *will convict the world* concerning sin and righteousness and judgment" (John 16:8, emphasis added). This is a declarative statement from a God who doesn't lie. So when he gives an invitation, it is given to people, knowing they have been drawn and convicted. So he can say, "*Come to me*, all who labor and are heavy laden, and I will give you rest" (Matthew 11:28, emphasis added).

How gracious it is that on the very last page of the Bible, his revelation to us of himself and his salvation, he inserts one more invitation to accept him and be saved. "And let the one who is thirsty *come*; let the one who desires take the water of life without price" (Revelation 22:17, emphasis added). How absurd then for Scripture to invite sinners to come and be saved if, not being one of the elect, it would be impossible for them to do so!

The Lord spent considerable time with Nicodemus, telling him about his need to be "born again," meaning to be regenerated. Nicodemus then asks the obvious question: "How can a man be born when he is old …? How can these things be?" (John 3:4, 9). Jesus's answer is clear. He gives the example of the bronze serpent lifted on a pole in the wilderness that saved people from the poisonous venom of the serpents' bites when they simply looked by faith. While the power of their healing came from God, it was their obedience to God's command that saved them. John 3:11 says, "That whoever *believes* in him may have eternal life" (emphasis added)—hence the gospel call: "Look and live!"

In summary, regeneration is indeed an act of God, but it is contingent on the willingness of the one desiring it to accept the gift. Faith is the response of a human being, with the God-given ability to choose, reaching out in true repentance to receive the gift offered by a loving God.

❖ How Is a Person Saved Today?

The simplicity of the way of salvation hasn't changed since first proclaimed after Christ rose from the dead. First, it requires that there be an acknowledgment of the existence of the holy Creator God and our accountability to him. Second, there must be an acknowledgment of our guilt before him because of our sin and going our own way and finally of our complete helplessness to fix the problem. Then in our lostness and guilt, we must turn to God and accept his gift of forgiveness available through the death of the Lord Jesus our Savior, choosing to follow him.

Paul gives us the theological summary of what is necessary in Romans 3. "For there is no distinction: for all have sinned and fall short of the glory of God and are *justified by his grace as a gift through the redemption that is in Christ Jesus*, whom God put forward *as a propitiation by his blood, to be received by faith*" (Romans 3:22–25, emphasis added).

1. Salvation is needed by all.
2. We are justified by his grace as a gift because of God's love.

3. Our redemption is by the sacrifice and death of Christ on the cross.
4. This fully satisfies God's holiness regarding our sin.
5. It is appropriated personally by the sinner through repentance and faith in Christ,

By our free will, we can refuse this priceless gift or receive it. The choice is ours. It might be somewhat likened to a conquered rebellious medieval knight coming and kneeling before the victorious king, throwing himself on the king's mercy, and pledging his allegiance. In reality, we open our hearts in acceptance, or we pray, acknowledging our need and accepting the Lord Jesus as Savior.

❖ If a Person Chooses Christ, Can He Then Later Choose Not to Believe? Would He Then Be Lost?

Please review the points on eternal security in chapter 3 in the section "Eternal Security" as well as in chapter 5 in the section "Who We Are as Being 'in Christ'—Forgiven and Now Adopted into His Family." Our salvation doesn't just consist of us simply coming to an understanding on our part of being lost and in repentance choosing (by free will) to accept Jesus as Savior. Or said differently, it is not just a one-sided, intellectual exercise on our part, for in that case, we might at some point, of course, just choose to walk away from Christ and the gospel.

However, having freely chosen to open our hearts to the Lord, then at that instance a God-empowered eternal transformation occurs, and we are judicially cleansed of all our sin once and for all, and are given new spiritual life, *eternal* life, and indwelt and empowered by God's Spirit. Yes, we still have a sin nature (in some older translations called "the flesh") within, giving us the propensity to sin although no longer the necessity of sinning. But in Romans 6 Paul counsels us to yield not to sin but to God (Romans 6:17–19), so sin no longer has absolute power over us. Also, we are born again and have been placed into God's family and given his promise that he will see us through to our full sanctification. To counteract the sin nature still within us, we now have

God's transforming Holy Spirit. See Ephesians 1, where we are told, "When you heard the word of truth, the gospel of your salvation, and believed in him, [you] were sealed with the promised Holy Spirit, who is the guarantee of our inheritance until we acquire possession of it" (Ephesians 1:13–14).

Also writing to these same believers later in his letter, Paul said, "And do not grieve the Holy Spirit of God, *by whom you were sealed for the day of redemption*" (Ephesians 4:30, emphasis added). So it is apparent that believers, who are "sealed for the day of redemption," may still choose to "walk in the flesh" (2 Corinthians 10:3), following their own desires without ever being abandoned by God. As Moses wrote in Numbers 23, "God is not man, that he should lie, or a son of man, that he should change his mind. Has he said, and will he not do it? Or has he spoken, and will he not fulfill it?" (Numbers 23:19).

Timothy was becoming somewhat overwhelmed and burned out while shepherding the church in Ephesus, so Paul wrote to encourage him to remain faithful. Because of the possibility of this younger man giving up on his task, Paul urged Timothy to "wage the good warfare, holding faith and a good conscience. By rejecting this, *some have made shipwreck of their faith*" (1 Timothy 1:18–20, emphasis added).

But this veering off course, making shipwreck, wasn't about losing or leaving one's salvation; it was about losing our joy and usefulness to God and our fellowship with him. Also, if we are truly God's children, then when we sin, the Lord will discipline us so we might return to full fellowship with him and his people and increase in our walk of holiness before him and the joy of his fellowship. "My son do not regard lightly the discipline of the Lord, nor be weary when reproved by him. For the Lord disciplines the one he loves and chastises every son whom he receives. It is for discipline that you have to endure. God is treating you as sons. For what son is there whom his father does not discipline? If you are left without discipline, in which all have participated, then you are illegitimate children and not sons" (Hebrews 12:5–9).

And if we are his children, we are totally secure in him. Jesus tells us, "*My sheep* hear my voice, and I know them, and they follow me. I give them *eternal life*, and *they will never perish*, and *no one will snatch them out of my hand*. My Father, who has given them to me, is greater than all, and no one is able to snatch them out of the Father's hand" (John 10:27–29, emphasis added).

But despite this reassurance, we can, though being in God's family, turn our backs on him and choose to live for ourselves. But be warned! Whether we turn away, God won't abandon even one of his children. He will in love discipline that person as we read above, and if he or she resolutely persists in rebellion, God will take him or her home to heaven. We see examples of this shortened life in the early church both in Jerusalem and in Corinth. But it is also very likely that a person who lives for years apart from God after turning away was never truly a believer but a hypocrite, a pretender (Greek, *hupokrites*), living for a while as if a believer but not truly being one. How difficult that must be! The base of this word comes from the Greek word meaning "to act." Some have sadly for some time done that acting very well. But in the end, as the apostle John wrote, "They went out from us, but they were not of us; for if they had been of us, they would have continued with us. But they went out, that it might become plain that they all are not of us" (1 John 2:19–20).

* ARE THERE TWO PARTS TO SALVATION—ACCEPTING JESUS AS SAVIOR AND NEEDING TO ACCEPT HIM AS LORD (SOMETIMES CALLED "LORDSHIP SALVATION")— FOR A PERSON TO TRULY BE SAVED?

Arthur W. Pink first propounded this view in the early part of the last century. He said, "No one can receive Christ as His Savior while he rejects Him as Lord. Therefore, those who have not bowed to Christ's scepter and enthroned Him in their hearts and lives, and yet imagine that they are trusting Him as Savior, are deceived."

John MacArthur has more recently further supported this view in his college and in his writings over the last number of decades. In his book *The Gospel According to Jesus*, John MacArthur champions Lordship salvation where he states "No one can come to Christ on any other term" than full commitment.[16]

Clarification here must involve looking at two aspects of the

Christian life—our salvation and our sanctification, our willingness to accept him as Savior and also allow Jesus to be Lord in our lives. First, look back earlier in this chapter to "How Is a Person Saved Today?" and what Paul says as he summarizes for us what salvation entails (especially in Romans 3:21–25).

As we saw, salvation involves a recognition of our sin, which causes us to fall short of God's glory; yet God graciously offers to us the gift of being justified before him because of Christ's work of redemption at Calvary. In repentance we accept it by faith; that's it! And we must not add to it.

If salvation was indeed in two parts, then we would also be taught in the Scriptures about the necessity of baptism for salvation. Baptism at its core is about giving testimony of Jesus's lordship in our lives. Certainly, we believers should all acknowledge Jesus as Lord in our lives and seek to live lives of discipleship before him. And we all should be baptized to present a witness of our salvation and commitment to live for Christ as Lord, but as Peter says, baptism doesn't save us. If God in Revelation 22 placed a curse on anyone who would add to the book, what judgment, do you suppose, would be due to the person adding to God's plan of salvation?

As to sanctification, however, Paul states when writing to the Christians in Rome, "Let not sin therefore reign in your mortal bodies, to make you obey their passions. Do not present your members to sin as instruments for unrighteousness but *present yourselves to God* [that's sanctification] as those who have been brought from death to life, and your members to God as instruments for righteousness" (Romans 6:12–13, emphasis added).

Presenting yourself to God is making him Lord of your life, saying, "Not my will but yours be done." At salvation we acknowledge his assessment of our guilt before him and that he is the Way. But now he desires that we live lives of obedience as well. Paul says this in the verse quoted above; as believers and "being alive" or having new life in Christ, we are now able, as we allow the Spirit to work in us, to resist sin. He doesn't call us to do the impossible. Paul tells us in Romans 8:4 to "*walk not according to the flesh but according* to the Spirit" (emphasis added). This may start as a first-time commitment, but it is something we need to do frequently and repeatedly throughout our lives. Paul speaks of this in Romans 12. "I appeal to you therefore, brothers, by the mercies of God, to present your bodies as a living sacrifice, holy and acceptable to God, which is your spiritual worship. Do not be conformed to this world, but *be transformed by the renewal of your mind*" (Romans 12:1–2, emphasis added).

Then again, he also says that being able to resist sin and live for God is a mark of the indwelling Spirit within us and of being saved. But yet it also is a day-by-day, minute-by-minute practice of allowing our will to be guided by the Spirit. See these verses in Romans 8. "If by the Spirit you put to death the deeds of the body, you will live. For all who are led by the Spirit of God are sons of God. For you did not receive the spirit of slavery to fall back into fear, but you have received the Spirit of adoption as sons, by whom we cry, 'Abba! Father!' The Spirit himself bears witness with our spirit that we are children of God" (Romans 8:13–17).

The witness spoken of here isn't just a feeling but the confidence that comes from seeing the working of God's power by the indwelling Spirit, which allows us to live this new life. And this new life will be a fulfillment of the plan God has for each believer by using the gifts of the Spirit for God's glory.

⬥ A Slightly Different Question Would Be: Are There Two Parts to Salvation—Accepting Jesus as Savior and Sometime Later Inviting the Holy Spirit to Indwell and Empower Us?

Salvation originated in the heart of the Father, was provided at Calvary by the Son, and comes individually to a person through the agency of the Holy Spirit when received by faith. John 3 below clearly tell us that the Holy Spirit births us into God's family. Then Romans 8 confirms that truth by saying that without the indwelling presence of God's Spirit, a person doesn't have God's salvation.

> Jesus answered, "Truly, truly, I say to you, unless one
> is born of water *and the Spirit*, he cannot enter the

kingdom of God. That which is born of the flesh is flesh, and that which is born of the Spirit is spirit." (John 3:5–6, emphasis added)

You, however, are not in the flesh but in the Spirit, if in fact the Spirit of God dwells in you. *Anyone who does not have the Spirit of Christ does not belong to him.* But if Christ is in you, although the body is dead because of sin, the Spirit is life because of righteousness. If the Spirit of him who raised Jesus from the dead dwells in you, he who raised Christ Jesus from the dead will also give life to your mortal bodies through his Spirit who dwells in you. (Romans 8:9–11, emphasis added)

The confusion comes, I believe, from not making a distinction between having the Spirit of God indwelling us, which occurs with our conversion, and additionally allowing him to lead as Lord of our lives and so allow us to walk in his power. The first has to do with a relationship, starting at the time of our salvation, and the second has to do with fellowship, which can change depending on the condition of our hearts and whether God is reigning in our lives. As an example, in Acts 2 we see the beginning of the church and all the believers in Jesus being indwelt with the Spirit of God. But then in Acts 4, with the looming threat of persecution, the believers earnestly prayed for boldness and God's power to be manifest. "They were all filled with the Holy Spirit." The result was that the Spirit already indwelling them was able to work powerfully in their lives. "And when they had prayed, the place in which they were gathered together was shaken, and they were all filled with the Holy Spirit and continued to speak the word of God with boldness" (Acts 4:31).

Practically then, in our Christian walk, there will no doubt be times when we become careless and self-centered in our lives, having unconfessed sin in our lives and certainly not allowing the Spirit of God to have control. Repenting of and confessing our sin, as John tells us in 1 John 1:9, is so important to restoring our fellowship with him and allowing his power to again work in our lives. This restoration, however, is not about being saved again. Be assured that when we become children of God, we are his forever. Nothing can separate us from his love.

◆ MUST A PERSON COME TO A POINT OF RESIGNATION OF BEING FOREVER LOST BEFORE GOD CAN SUPERNATURALLY OPEN THE PERSON'S EYES TO THE GIFT OF HIS SALVATION?

I thought when I was young that salvation was something like God just turning a light on. I suppose that this particular way of telling the story of one's personal salvation, which I had heard so frequently while growing up, grew out of a concern for people making so-called false professions, a concern about an "easy believism." I recall many instances of people who previously made a profession of salvation and had subsequently been baptized. But later, usually during a series of gospel meetings, they became convicted about their sin and how they were living. As a result, they again prayed a prayer of confession and acceptance of Jesus as Savior. We cannot know a person's heart, but no doubt in most of these cases, these people, though truly saved, hadn't been living for the Lord or acknowledging his lordship in their lives. But with not having been invited to take the step of receiving Christ when they were desiring God's salvation, they were left with doubts.

This question given above has in it the flavor of Calvinism with the suggestion that, once we are sufficiently repentant, then God will by his power open our eyes to the realization that we are saved, but this approach seems to skip the step of exercising our faith by a personal act of receiving Christ as our Savior. Certainly, there must be a clear recognition of need and a change of heart, of conviction. Then in repentance, there is a turning to God to receive his gift. That's salvation.

On the other hand, there may be those who, at the initial time of their so-called salvation, really did just go through the motions to satisfy others or even to get them to stop evangelizing them. But Peter, on the day of Pentecost and after the people were convicted of their sin, told them what they must do to be saved. He closed his first great gospel message by saying, "And it shall come to pass that *everyone who calls upon the name of the Lord shall be saved*" (Acts 2:21, emphasis added). Also see this story about the Philippian jailer and what Paul told him. "And the jailer called for lights and rushed in and trembling with fear he fell down before Paul and Silas. Then he brought them out and said, 'Sirs, what must I do to be saved?' And they said, *'Believe in the Lord Jesus, and you will be saved,* you and your household'" (Acts 16:29–32, emphasis added).

This insistence on a sudden additional "illumination" would suggest a belief, held by some, in the necessity of spiritual regeneration by God <u>before</u> we receive Christ as Savior, which isn't a doctrine found in Scripture. Instead, we see these people being convicted or illuminated by the Holy Spirit of their sin through hearing the gospel, then needing to take the active step of believing in and receiving the Lord Jesus as their Savior. God then does his miraculous work of making us new creations in Christ Jesus.

To clarify, when God told Adam he would die if he ate of the forbidden fruit and Paul in Ephesians 2 said that before their salvation these Ephesians were "dead in their sins," they weren't referring to a loss of characteristics that mark us as human beings made in God's image. Nor did those acts negate our moral consciences or free will. What they did do is sever us from a relationship with our Creator, allowing Satan to have dominion over us. We continue, though spiritually dead, to be responsible for the way we live our lives and to personally take the step of putting our faith in Christ for our salvation.

❖ Can We know for Sure That We're Eternally Saved?

First, we must depend on the infallible Word of God telling us so, and we also must put our reliance on the very character of God, who has said so. Also, we are assured of this based on the efficacy of the person and work of our Lord Jesus Christ. Certainly, God the Father was fully satisfied by the Lord's sacrifice at Calvary, which he showed by raising him from the dead. Paul explains that this power is now at work in us, and we are secure in God. He speaks of "the immeasurable greatness of his power toward us who believe, according to the working of his great might that he worked in Christ when he raised him from the dead and seated him at his right hand in the heavenly places" (Ephesians 1:19–20).

Would we call God a liar or untrustworthy in what he has promised? See Hebrews 7, quoted earlier, which speaks to us of the length of time for which our salvation is effective. "The former priests were many in number, because they were prevented by death from continuing in office, but *he holds his priesthood permanently, because he continues forever.* Consequently, *he is able to save to the uttermost those who draw near to God through him,* since *he always lives* to make intercession for them" (Hebrews 7:23–25, emphasis added).

The apostle John was sure that a person who had accepted Christ as Savior could have this assurance when he wrote, "Whoever has the Son has life; whoever does not have the Son of God does not have life. I write these things to you who believe in the name of the Son of God *that you may know that you have eternal life*" (1 John 5:12–14, emphasis added).

The Greek tenses here in this last phrase are instructive. The first word is *know* and is in the perfect tense, speaking of *a current condition based on a past completed action.* The second word *have* is in the present tense, meaning *something we currently possess.* The preciseness of the Greek language John used was certainly helpful to those he was writing to as he refuted heretical beliefs creeping into their church. And it remains so for us today.

Connected to the truth of being eternally saved is our personal assurance that this is true. See the next question below.

◆ What if We Struggle with Assurance? Does That Mean We Aren't Really Saved?

First, let it be said that every believer can have doubts—doubting is human. This is an internal struggle and is really about our thinking and feelings. These doubts are from Satan. But assurance will come from the Scripture and from learning about the trustworthiness of our God as well as from seeing the Lord work in our lives. Perhaps you were taught unbiblical doctrine when growing up. Or perhaps this struggle actually comes because of doubts about God's character. Is he genuinely good and trustworthy? Do you believe he has let you down? Remember, we are living in a world under Satan's control, and bad things do happen to good people, but these aren't a surprise to God. He is still in ultimate control, and God will make something truly good come out of all our troubles as we rely on him. See this verse below as well as the text from 1 John 5 above that can give us real assurance of God's plans for us.

Perhaps you'd like to write these verses out to remind yourself of God's faithfulness. Also, because we forget so easily, it would be good to start the habit of writing down each time you receive a blessing from God. You will be surprised at how often this happens. Despite our current situation, make another habit of reminding yourself of the future God has promised to you. "In him you also, when you heard the word of truth, the gospel of your salvation, and believed in him, were sealed with the promised Holy Spirit, who is the guarantee of our inheritance until we acquire possession of it, to the praise of his glory" (Ephesians 1:13–14).

What happens when we sin as believers? Certainly, sin may make us doubt our salvation, and we may lose our joy. But the apostle John, speaking to believers, answers this question clearly in 1 John 1:8–9, as quoted previously. "If we confess our sins, he is faithful and just to forgive us our sins and to cleanse us from all unrighteousness." Also, we will feel the guilt of this sin more keenly than as an unbeliever. But then, John says, if we confess, we are forgiven.

Finally, we know and can be assured of God's love for us as his children because he was willing to allow his Son to die for us. Certainly, we can't see the big picture, and the way for us in this world may be very hard; but never forget. "He who promised is faithful" (Hebrews 10:23). He has given us his word. To doubt then is to doubt his character.

◆ FINALLY, IS BAPTISM A NECESSARY PART OF OUR SALVATION?

Certainly, baptism is one of the two ordinances (symbolic acts) given to the church that were carried out by believers from the very beginning of church history starting in Jerusalem. All who put their trust in the Lord Jesus ought to testify to this new reality by being baptized. So baptism remains necessary as an act of obedience but not as part of our salvation, introducing even the smallest amount of work into it. Acts 2:42, which summarizes the continuing activities of the early church, doesn't mention baptism since anyone identifying himself or herself as part of the church would certainly have already been baptized with no need for baptism to be repeated.

In the Scripture, we see that God takes symbolism seriously more so than we do today. Remember Moses striking the rock twice instead of once, as the Lord had asked? By doing so, he marred the picture of Christ needing to be stuck only once at Calvary for our sins and never again. God disciplined Moses and didn't allow him to enter the Promised Land.

However, when we speak directly to this symbol of baptism, it is also important for us not to add anything to the meaning God intended. In Romans 6:3–4, Paul spells out for us the meaning of this act. "Do you not know that all of us who have been baptized into Christ Jesus were baptized into his death? We were buried therefore with him by baptism into death, in order that, just as Christ was raised from the dead by the glory of the Father, *we too might walk in newness of life*" (emphasis added).

Baptism's essential meaning was to publicly proclaim as believers our identification with Christ as both our Savior and the Lord of our lives. It also proclaimed our dying to our wills and desires and committing ourselves to living new lives for God's glory.

In some churches, there actually is a prepared baptismal tank filled with water at every service, so if someone professes salvation, that person can immediately be baptized. The person would do this practice based on his or her belief that salvation involves both faith plus baptism. He or she sees this from Peter's sermon in Acts 2:38 and Mark 16:16, although there are strong indications that these last few verses of Mark's Gospel weren't part of the original manuscripts.

Also note Paul's words in Romans 4, where he speaks of Abraham's circumcision—an important sign of Jewish identification with Jehovah God. But Paul says it wasn't the "work" of circumcision that brought Abraham into fellowship with God; it was his faith occurring before circumcision.

Since I brought up the topic of circumcision, it is appropriate to briefly mention here that circumcision is *not* a Christian rite. As a physician, I would certainly say it can be very beneficial medically, but once we give it a spiritual connotation, it sinks to the level of works if connecting it in any way to our salvation. In the Old Testament, its significance was as a national identity for the Jewish people. It's not prescribed in the New Testament for believers or their children, and it becomes a form of legalism.

Continuing on the topic of baptism, we see that the thief on the cross was not baptized, yet Jesus promised that he would be with the Lord in paradise. Luke 23:42–43 says, "And he said, 'Jesus, remember me when you come into your kingdom.' And he said to him, 'Truly, I say to you, today you will be with me in Paradise.'"

In addition, coming back to Peter, we see him speaking of baptism in his first epistle, in which he makes a distinction between salvation and the expected obedience of a believer to Jesus as his Lord. Here in 1 Peter 3:21–22 we read, "Baptism, which corresponds to this, now saves you (not the removal of the filth of the flesh, but the pledge of a good conscience toward God) through the resurrection of Jesus Christ" (Holman Christian Standard Bible).

First, note that the words in parentheses in this verse are included as part of the original text. Also note that the word *this,* from a grammatical point of view, is referring back to the phrase in verse 18. "Put to death in the flesh but made alive in the spirit" initially refers to our Lord but now is being applied by Peter to us who are being baptized—dying to self but now alive to God. As a Christian, is the Lord Jesus the Lord of your life?

Also, the use of the word *flesh* in this verse corresponds, I believe, to the context of how Paul used it in Romans 8, speaking of the sin nature or self-will within us rather than actual dirt on a person's physical body. "To set the mind on the flesh is death, but to set the mind on the Spirit is life and peace. For the mind that is set on the flesh is hostile to God, for it does not submit to God's law; indeed, it cannot. Those, who are in the flesh [i.e., self-willed and living for themselves], cannot please God" (Romans 8:6–8).

In contrast, Jesus, when in the upper room washing his disciples' feet, told Peter that having a complete bath wasn't necessary, since as a man of faith, he had already had his sins washed away. The symbolism of a bath in that instance spoke about salvation.

Also, saying that baptism doesn't save us doesn't mean it's not essential for believers' obedience and testimony. It is one of the two church ordinances, along with the Lord's Supper, given to us in the New Testament and was to be performed by a person upon receiving Christ as Savior. That's why Peter speaks of it as being important for a good conscience. We see what happened on the day of Pentecost, as Luke recorded this momentous event. "So those who received his word were baptized, and there were added that day about three thousand souls" (Acts 2:41).

Symbolically then, a believer's baptism is important to God, and it is one of those symbols to which we must continue to be committed. Besides being a public witness to our faith in Christ, it is also a lordship issue (see Romans 6), a public commitment of oneself to live for God. Going down into the water typifies the death of our wills, and by coming up out of the water, we are publicly committing ourselves to live as new persons with wills that are submissive to the Lord Jesus. Let us remember this commitment before God for the rest of our lives.

Chapter Seven

Comparative Religions Addendum

Going back to the beginning of our study, we saw that the deepest universal need in us as human beings is to deal with the problem of our estrangement from our Creator, our feelings of personal guilt at not being fit to come before him, and our desire to try in some way to atone for it. We are all searchers, not necessarily for truth, desiring to find the right way, but at its core, this is for absolution and restoration of fellowship with God.

How wonderful it is that the Christian faith, as given to us in the Scriptures, reveals to us God's plan of salvation that, to use a modern colloquial expression, ticks off all the boxes and more besides! We're given the reasons for desiring to reconnect with our Creator. He made us that way, made in his image, with the echo of what once was and what we desire to reclaim, still within us. The weight of the guilt of our sin is revealed to us as not being just a psychological maladjustment but a very real need with consequent judgment ahead. Also, God's moral code, based on his essential character, has been imprinted on every heart—so we feel guilty because, in fact, we are! We fall short. But then, compared to other religions, Scripture reveals to us something wholly new—God's love for us and his desire to forgive us based on his sacrifice, not on our efforts. You would search in vain to find this in any of the thousands of other non-Christian belief systems.

But this salvation goes much further than forgiveness, great as that is. God's plan is that, having been saved from our sins, we might then be changed to become like him—holy and blameless and so fit to be in his presence. Unlike other religions, in which remaining in good standing with God is based on our obedience and adherence to God's commandments, the Bible tells us that upon acceptance of Jesus Christ as Savior, we are adopted into his family and given a guarantee by his Spirit's presence within us of being eternally secure in him. So much more than being just a religion, it's a relationship.

Other religions teach that we must do good works to earn God's favor but certainly without any guarantee of attaining it or understanding how much would be enough. God's Word says we should do good works to show our appreciation for the gift of salvation he gives us. And so many people in this world continue to toil through life under what they believe is the rather malevolent eye of One who will judge them. It's a heavy and truly impossible task.

The great difference then in the gospel message given to us in Scripture is its teaching that our holy God actually loves us. Our salvation is not merit based, as we learn from Paul in Romans 5:8. "God shows his love for us in that while we were still sinners, Christ died for us." It's his free gift to all who put their faith in Jesus (Ephesians 2:9).

This makes all the difference and brings into focus the other gracious gifts and plans he has for us. As we're told in Ephesians 1, we're given forgiveness of our sin, accepted into his family, gifted the promise of being made fully holy and blameless, and given eternal life in fellowship with God and the sure promise of heaven. Nothing else comes close to this. It's more than we could have ever asked or even hoped for!

This reminds me of the booklet an old evangelist gave me shortly after I was saved. It was titled *Safety, Certainty and Enjoyment*, and it was written early in the last century by George Cutting. Its message was a simple one based on verses taken from Scripture and meant to reassure a person that once we are in the safety of God's hands, according to the truth of his Word, we are truly secure, eternally so, and have every right to live from then on in the certainty and enjoyment of sins forgiven.

God's Word is the solid rock of unchanging truth we can stand on. One of the verses in that book was from the apostle John at the end of his first epistle, written to encourage believers, about this same truth. "I write these things to you who believe in the name of the Son of God *that you may know that you have eternal life*" (1 John 5:13, emphasis added).

The word *have* in this verse is in the Greek, present tense; it emphasizes a present reality. And "know" is in the perfect tense, speaking to a present reality based on a past completed action.[17]

What was true when John wrote this at the end of the first century remains as true today as then. It's a hope unique to the Christian faith, so let us rejoice and be glad in it. We have, as believers in the Lord Jesus Christ, been justified through Christ, regenerated by the Spirit, reconciled before God, and adopted into his eternal family. God in his Word guarantees it. It can't get better than that!

Chapter Eight

Conclusion

Concerning the Lord and the greatness of his work on our behalf, John writes at the conclusion of his Gospel (just after Thomas saw the risen Lord and exclaimed, "My Lord and my God"), that Jesus "did many other signs" and then finishes by saying, "But these are written so that you may believe that Jesus is the Christ, the Son of God, and that by believing you may have life [salvation and spiritual life] in his name" (John 20:31).

So, in essence, his Gospel is a treatise on the good news of salvation, showing us that Jesus was the One sent from God and was, in fact, the eternal Son of God and that through him and only through him we have eternal life. The writer of Hebrews 2:3 calls this reconciliation of man to God "so great a salvation," and indeed it is!

But we have seen that, spurred on by Satan, men and women in every generation, have tried to add their own efforts to God's fully sufficient work. It is my prayer that in this matter of being "made right with God" we might shed the encrustations of the past and return to the profound simplicity of God's Word, putting our faith solely in the finished work of our Lord Jesus Christ.

Scripture tells us that God is holy in the very essence of his being and that God is love, a core characteristic of his person. Yet in his profound wisdom, God found a way to remain perfectly holy and yet able to express his super-abounding love by redeeming us and buying us back to himself, rebellious sinners though we were. Beyond that, he has shown us that he has in his sovereign will called us to himself as a people with whom he can be in an eternal relationship, pictured as his bride. At the same time, he allows these same ones he so loves to, of their own free will, choose to trust in and follow him and be a part of his plans in a coming future. Hallelujah!

We need to worship the Lord our God for the greatness of his person, the majesty of his creation, and particularly the creation of humanity, made in his image. What an amazing thing he has done! But supremely we must worship him and give him glory because of the grandeur of his reconciling work of redeeming us back to himself. All praise to God that we are reunited with him because of his work of love accomplished through that great and perfect plan of salvation.

Soli Deo gloria!

Acknowledgments

I so appreciate the many people who have given of their time to make corrections and helpful suggestions while I was writing this book. Thank you to Brian Stapley, a friend for many years, retired secondary school teacher, and director of the Boys JIM Club of America, for helping me to improve my writing and for that first editing run-through. Also a thank you to Leigh Hartley, again a long-time Christian friend, for providing a number of insightful comments and pushing me to more carefully clarify my desire and purpose in writing this book. Thanks as well to Peter Kerr particularly for his encouragement and for urging me to have this book published. Peter has had an itinerant preaching ministry for many years in southern Ontario, where he was also a lecturer at Kawartha Lakes Bible College. Currently, he is the Canadian Director of the Emmaus Correspondence School for Canada. In addition I am grateful to Don Salmans, ThM, also a past lecturer at KLBC for several helpful suggestions. Finally, I am very grateful to my wife, Gayle, for her ongoing encouragement and who spent hours reading the manuscript and making so many helpful suggestions.

I am most thankful for the Lord, who put it in my heart to embark on this task. I have ended the book above with the Latin inscription *soli Deo gloria*, and that is my prayer. May the glory go to God, my Savior, alone.

Endnotes

1 *A Faith to Confess: The Baptist Confession of 1689, Rewritten in Modern English,* Section 3:3 (Carey Publications, 1997).

2 John C. Lennox, *God's Undertaker: Has Science Buried God?* (Lion Hudson Place, 2009).

3 *Dictionary.com,* registered May 14, 1995, based on Random House Unabridged Dictionary

4 W. E. Vine, *Expository Dictionary of New Testament Words,* 19th ed. (London: Oliphants, 1940, 1969), Vol III, p.316

5 *The Boy Who Lost His Boat* (Good News Publishers, 2000).

6 John Bunyan, *Pilgrim's Progress* (initially written in 1676). Oliver Hunkin rewrote it in more modern English in 1985 as *Dangerous Journey* (Marshall Morgan and Scott), 40.

7 Harold W. Hoehner, *Ephesians, An Exegetical Commentary,* Baker Academic, 2002, p.342

8 Billy Graham, *Just As I Am, The Autobiography of Billy Graham,* HarperCollins Pub. P.138-139

9 The Nicene Creed (First Council of Nicaea in AD 325, written largely by Athanasia).

10 David R. Anderson, *Free Grace Soteriology* (Xulon Press, 2010), 138.

11 William MacDonald, *Believer's Bible Commentary, New Testament* (A & O Press, 1989).

12 Rob Bell, *Love Wins* (HarperCollins, 2011), 140–141.

13 Don Richardson, *Peace Child* (G/L Publications, 1974).

14 Council of Trent, 1545–63 (Session VI, Can. 12).

15 Matt Papa, *Look and Live* (Bethany House, 2014), 41.

16 John MacArthur, *The Gospel According to Jesus,* (Zondervan, 1988, 1994), p. 197

17 Buist M. Fanning, *Verbal Aspect in New Testament Greek* (Oxford Theology and Religion Monographs) (1991-01-17), 290–91.

Bibliography

P. A. Kerr, *Election and Predestination: Looking for Answers Not Arguments* (Everyday Publications, 2020).

Ronald E. Showers, *There Really Is a Difference: A Comparison of Covenant and Dispensational Theology*, 13th ed. (Friends of Israel Gospel Ministry, 2013).

The Brown-Driver-Briggs-Gesenius Hebrew and English Lexicon.

Thayer's Greek Lexicon (transliterated).

Dudley Ward, *Programmed by God or Free to Choose? Five-Point Calvinism under the Searchlight* (Eugene, OR: Resource Publications, 2008).

Printed in the United States
by Baker & Taylor Publisher Services